D1629804

Church's Story 3

The Church's Story
Lived by the People of God

Acknowledgements
There have been many contributors to the contents of this book. The Primary Religious Education Advisers (past and present) from the Dioceses of England and Wales have been tireless in their enthusiasm in drafting and re-drafting its contents. They are a generous group of people who deserve our thanks and appreciation for their faithfulness and commitment.

Even with their efforts this book would not have come to fruition had it not been for the inspiration, imagination and dedication of the former coordinator for *Living and Sharing our Faith: a National Project for catechesis and Religious Education*, Anne White, whose generosity in sharing her wisdom and experience has been much appreciated by the present coordinator. Her work for 'the Project' has been constant and thorough and she leaves a rich legacy for the children, young people and adults who will come to use these resources. We owe her a debt of gratitude for the service she offers the Church and her part in its Story.

Church's Story 3

A National Project of Catechesis and Religious Education Publication

Published by Rejoice Publications
an imprint of
Matthew James Publishing Ltd,
19 Wellington Close,
Chelmsford, Essex CM1 2EE

ISBN 1 899481 24 9

First published 2006

Nihil Obstat: Mgr George Stokes, Censor
Imprimatur: Rt Rev Thomas McMahon, Bishop of Brentwood
Brentwood, 9 May 2006

The Nihil obstat and Imprimatur are a declaration that a book or pamphlet is considered to be free from doctrinal or moral error. It is not implied that those who have granted the Nihil obstat or Imprimatur agree with the contents, opinions or statements expressed.

Design and page layout by Gill England
Printed in China for Compass Press Ltd

Contents

Welcome

Dear Children,

In this book you will discover the Church's Story. This is a story which began when Jesus asked his friends to continue to do the things he had shown them. It is a story which is written here, but continues in the people around us today. You are a part of that story.

Every day the story is retold and celebrated. All the People of God are invited to this celebration to remember Jesus and the things he taught us through the things he did and the things he said. These things help us to love one another. They are like gifts from Jesus. We show we have these gifts when we help someone, say we are sorry, share the things we have and keep our promises.

Sometimes the people of God have celebrations to remember special times in the life of Jesus and his friends. These are part of the Church's Story. Telling the story to each other helps us to remember. One day your children may tell this story about you.

† Edwin Regan
Bishop of Wrexham
Chairman of the National Project

The People of God

This book tells the story of the Church.

The Church is a community of Christian believers. Everyone who is baptised in the name of the Father, and of the Son and of the Holy Spirit belongs to this community. Everyone who searches for love and truth by listening to the Spirit of God belongs to this community.

You will discover that the Church is found in families and communities which make up a worldwide family of believers.

You will read about the Church's sacraments which celebrate the love and life of God shared through Jesus.

You will learn about the seasons and feasts of the Church's year.

All through the book you will find references to God's Story 3. In that book you can read more about the story of God's love told by the People of God of the Old and New Testaments.

Jesus said 'I am the vine and you are the branches.'

We, who are many, are one body in Christ,
and we are members one of another.

In the Beginning

Before the world was made there was God.

The Bible begins with the book of Genesis, which is a beautiful story of how our world came into being at God's word.

God's life-giving Spirit brought all creation into being.

The entire universe is God's work.

All created things have life as God's gift.

One book of the Bible is a collection of psalms, inspired songs to God.

Some psalms celebrate God's creative nature. Their authors see God's work in the world around them.

My God how great you are!

You made the moon to mark the seasons;
The sun knows when to set.
Some animals come out only at night
To find the food that you provide.
The sun rises and they go back to sleep.......

What wonders you do in the world.
They are far too many to count.
The world is full of your creatures........
You provide the food they gather;
Your open hand gives them their fill.
My God how great you are!

(Based on Psalm 104: 10-30.
See God's Story 3 p.51)

'Some animals come out only at night to find the food that you provide.'

'The world is full of your creatures...'

Bible

The Bible is the story of God's love and how, through its history, God's People have responded to that love. For Christians, the Bible is God's word. (In God's Story 3 you will find more of this story.)

The Books of the Bible known to Christians as the Old Testament are the Hebrew Scriptures for Jewish people. 'Scriptures' means 'writings'.

In the New Testament, the Gospels tell of Jesus and his mission to tell everyone the Good News of God his Father. Listening to stories and readings from the Bible helps the Christian family to stay close to God. God's Word is proclaimed when Christians gather for prayer or worship. People also read the Bible on their own.

In a Court of Law when Christians testify that what they say is true they are given a Bible to make this promise.

(Books: Here I Am Years 3/4)

Called to Life

God calls each person to life.
Each one is fashioned in God's own image and likeness.

Each of us is alive with God's own life and love.

God wants each person to be aware of this life and love, so that they can share it with others.

God creates people.

God loves each person.

God's love is everlasting and unchanging.

I thank you and I praise you
For creating wonderful me!
Whilst I was in my mother's womb
You loved me and you knew me.
And now, Creator God,
you still watch me....
Even before I speak,
you know my words....
If I were to climb the highest mountain
You would be there....
Your thoughts and dreams for me
Are as many as the stars in heaven
And grains on the seashore.
I think you are just WONDERFUL!

(Based on Psalm 139 See God's Story 3 p.48)

UNIQUE

Each person is unique.

Unique in his or her family.

Unique in the world today.

Unique in history.

Christians believe that this uniqueness is evidence of the love of the Creator God.

Christians believe that one Person in all of human history is the most complete and unique revelation of God. This Person is Jesus.

Jesus is the Son of God, sent by his Father so that we would know God and how much God loves us. God became human in the person of Jesus. We call this the Incarnation.

Your iris and your finger prints are unique. Modern technology is making use of this uniqueness. Soon you will be able to be identified by machines that recognise your unique iris.

Jesus would have prayed the psalms. The Church uses these prayers to help people remember God's love is for always.

God is always there for me:

Always ready to help me when
I am in trouble.

Even when there are earthquakes,
storms and floods

I need not be afraid.

God is always with me,
sheltering me from harm.

God is with me all day.

(Based on Psalm 46:1, 2, 9, 11, 14, 15, 19, 22-24. (See God's Story 3 p.46)

JESUS AND THE CHURCH

In the gospels, we read how Jesus always fulfilled what his Father asked of him. In his human life he reveals not only what God is like but how we are to live as children of God.

Jesus invited people to follow him and learn a new way of life. He invited them to become one family, one in love of each other and one in the love of his Father and the Holy Spirit.

In the first century after the resurrection of Jesus his followers began to be called Christians. The assembly of believers was called 'church'.

Where will you find the Church?

"Love one another as I have loved you."

"Love your neighbour."

"Forgive us our trespasses as we forgive those who trespass against us."

"Hallowed be your name."

"Your will be done."

"Go out to the whole world. Proclaim the Good News."

How will you know Christians?

At home...

In the neighbourhood...

In the world...

A New Way of Living

The gospels are evidence of how the early Church believed that being a disciple of Jesus meant living in a new way.

From the Gospel of Matthew:
"Love your enemies and pray for those who bully you.
If you do this, you will be sons and daughters of God your Father in heaven."

"God's love is like the sun which rises each day and gives warmth and light to everyone, not just to good people...
I tell you your love must be like God's love."

"God loves everyone no matter who they are or what they do. You must not put any limits on your love, for the love of your Father in heaven is never ending, never changing."

(Based on the Gospel of Matthew 5:44-48. See God's Story 3 p.84. Here I Am, Homes and Families Years 5/6)

FAMILY LIFE

God's Joy
Sing and shout for joy.
Rejoice with all your heart.
The Lord, the king of Israel,
is with you;
There is no reason now to be afraid.
The Lord your God is with you.
The Lord will take delight in you
And in his love he will give you
new life.
He will sing and be joyful over you,
As joyful as a people at a festival.
The time is coming.
See God's Story 3 p.67
"God Sings for Joy".

Each person is created by God to be born into a family. It can be a very large family or a very small family. A family lives together and shares a way of life. Each family is unique and different.

It is within a family that we first learn about ourselves and our world. It is through family life with its joys, sorrows and challenges that we learn about God's wish for us to be loving and forgiving, just as God is to each one of us. When we share this love and show it in many ways within our world we are reflecting God's love in creation.

Sometimes the family is described as the 'Domestic Church' that is to say the Church in the home.

God's Loving Forgiveness

Jesus told many stories to help his friends understand difficult things. His parables are stories with a special meaning. They are like puzzles so that when you read them you have to think and try to work out the message that Jesus gives to his friends today.

You will find one of the most memorable parables in the gospel according to Luke. It is the parable of the prodigal son.
(See God's Story 3 pp102-103)

Through this story, Jesus is telling us what God his Father is like. Some people think the story should really have the title 'The Prodigal Father'. Can you think why?

(Homes and Families, Here I Am Years 5/6)

STEWARDS OF CREATION

God called the world into being and continues this creative action every day.

God invites each one of us to share in the continuing work of creation throughout the whole of our lives.

We call this work of looking after creation 'Stewardship'.

> *Look after the world;*
> *look after one another;*
> *take care of the fish and the birds,*
> *the animals and the reptiles,*
> *the trees and the flowers and the plants.*
> *(Based on Genesis 1:30)*

As stewards of creation we share the privilege and responsibility of caring for our world and all the people in it. The choices we make to reflect God's love help us transform the world into the place God intends it to be.

Above: Recycling bank in Egypt
Above left: A proud gardener with his home-grown strawberries
Left: A street cleaner in Vietnam

Top: Volunteers at Llannelli Wildlife and Wetland Centre caring for birds caught in an oil spill in Swansea Bay.
Top right: Wind Farm in East Anglia
Above right: Harvesting rice in Vietnam
Right: Model of a zebra made from recycled keyboards

The Church family has particular ways of continuing the work of creation.

Different organisations are concerned with care of the environment, and the needs of God's people across the world. Two of the organisations that reflects our call to stewardship are CAFOD and Mission Together.

Mission Together Prayer

We pray
May all children
In the world
Share love
Share friendship and live
In the peace
Of God's love
Now and forever
Amen

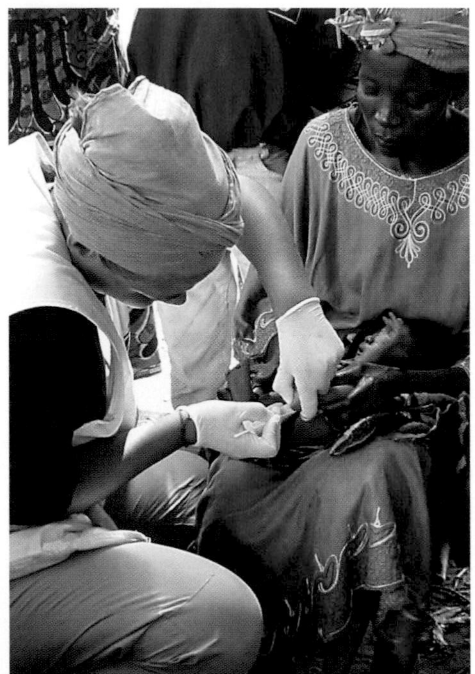

CAFOD is the official agency of the Catholic Church. It works in partnership alongside people in need to reduce poverty and bring about sustainable change. CAFOD believes the goods of creation are developed and shared by all, rich and poor alike. Their website is at **www.cafod.org.uk**

Based on the motto 'Children Helping Children', **Mission Together** encourages a concern for children world-wide by prayer, learning activities and fund-raising. Their website is at **www.missiontogether.org.uk**

CAFOD works on long term projects to ensure that all people have access to food, clean water, shelter and security, health and education.

TELL THE GOOD NEWS

In the gospels, we read about Jesus' mission. 'Gospel' means 'Good News'. The good news Jesus came to make known is that God loves each of us and that living God's Way brings love, justice and peace for all the world.

Jesus chose people to be apostles and share his mission. 'Apostle' means 'one who is sent'. We read in the gospels that Jesus named twelve people to be the first apostles and help him tell others the good news of God.

Friends of Jesus

You can read more about some of the apostles Jesus chose in Friends of Jesus by Victoria Hummell ra. (McCrimmons 2003)

Through the sacrament of Baptism all Christians are called to share in the mission of Jesus. There are many different ways of carrying out this mission.

God calls each of us to a particular vocation in life. 'Vocation' means 'calling'. Some people's vocation is to marriage, the single life or religious life. These are the laity.

Some people's vocation is to ordination as a deacon, priest or bishop. Within these vocations there are many different ways of living out the mission of Jesus day by day. Each one has an important but different role in the mission of the Church.

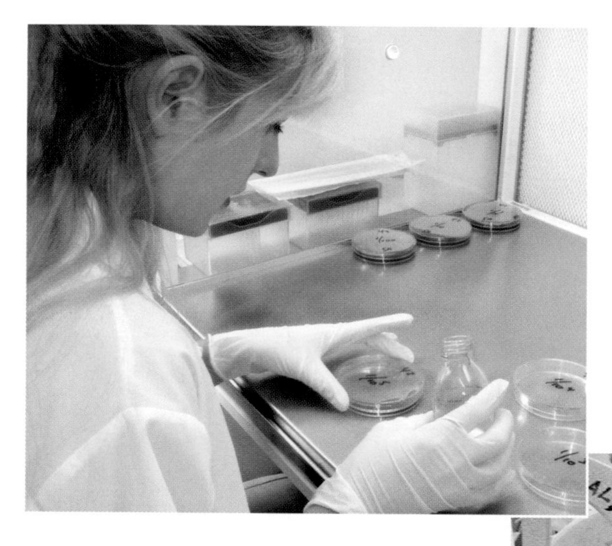

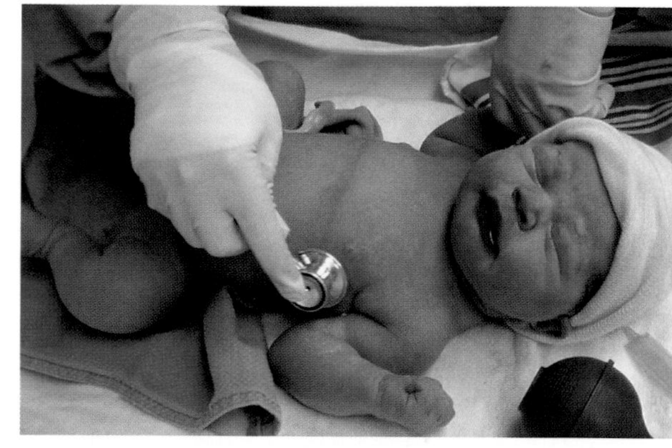

Which of these is a life-long vocation?

Which of these is a Christian vocation?

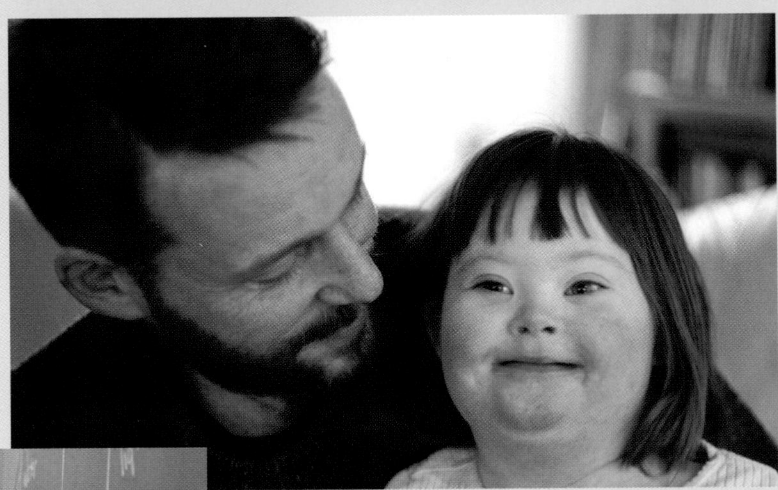

PARISH LIFE

A parish is a Christian community in a geographical area. A parish church is where the community gathers.

THE LAITY

Lay people of all ages serve in their parishes in different ways. They help build up the community of the parish where people are cared for and serve others as Jesus commanded.

Find Out

Where is your parish church?

Who are the ordained ministers in your parish?

What is the name of your parish?

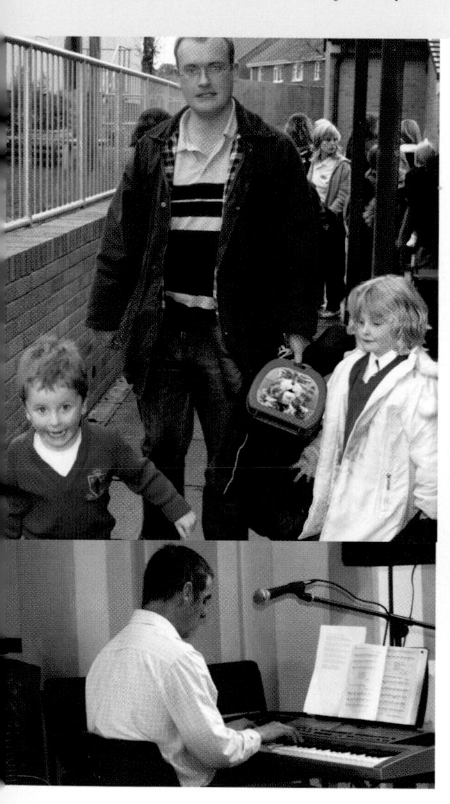

ORDAINED MINISTERS

In the parish family the priest carries out the ministry of leading the celebration of the sacraments. He will also visit the sick, the schools and other members of the parish family. There may be more than one priest in a parish. Some parishes have a deacon who is ordained to administer some sacraments and to care for and serve the people.

What do you think?

Cardinal John Henry Newman, a famous 19th century preacher and writer, was asked "Who are the laity?" He said, "The Church would look foolish without them."

The Diocese

Above: Bishop Edwin Regan, Bishop of Wrexham, with a Carmelite Sister on the occasion of her Solemn Profession at the Carmelite Monastery in Dolgellau, Wales

Find Out

What is the name of your Bishop?

What is the name of your diocese?

Where is the cathedral of your diocese?

How many bishops are there in England and Wales?

THE BISHOP

A Diocese is made up of many parishes.

The Bishop leads the Christian family in his Diocese.

The main church in a diocese is called a Cathedral. 'Cathedral' comes from a Latin word meaning 'seat' so the cathedral is where the diocesan bishop has his 'seat'. This is the symbol of his responsibility and authority and he takes his seat here when he celebrates Mass. Bishops are the successors of the Apostles.

The role of the Bishop is to unite all the parish families within a diocese. He does this through visiting each parish, celebrating confirmation, ordaining men to the priesthood and diaconate and proclaiming the Gospel. He is like a shepherd in the way he looks after and cares for his people as a shepherd cares for his sheep.

The mitre is worn on his head and symbolises the two sources of his authority – the Bible and the Church.

The cross shows he walks in the footsteps of Christ.

The ring shows he is faithful to God and to leading his people.

The crozier is a symbol of how he is like a shepherd.

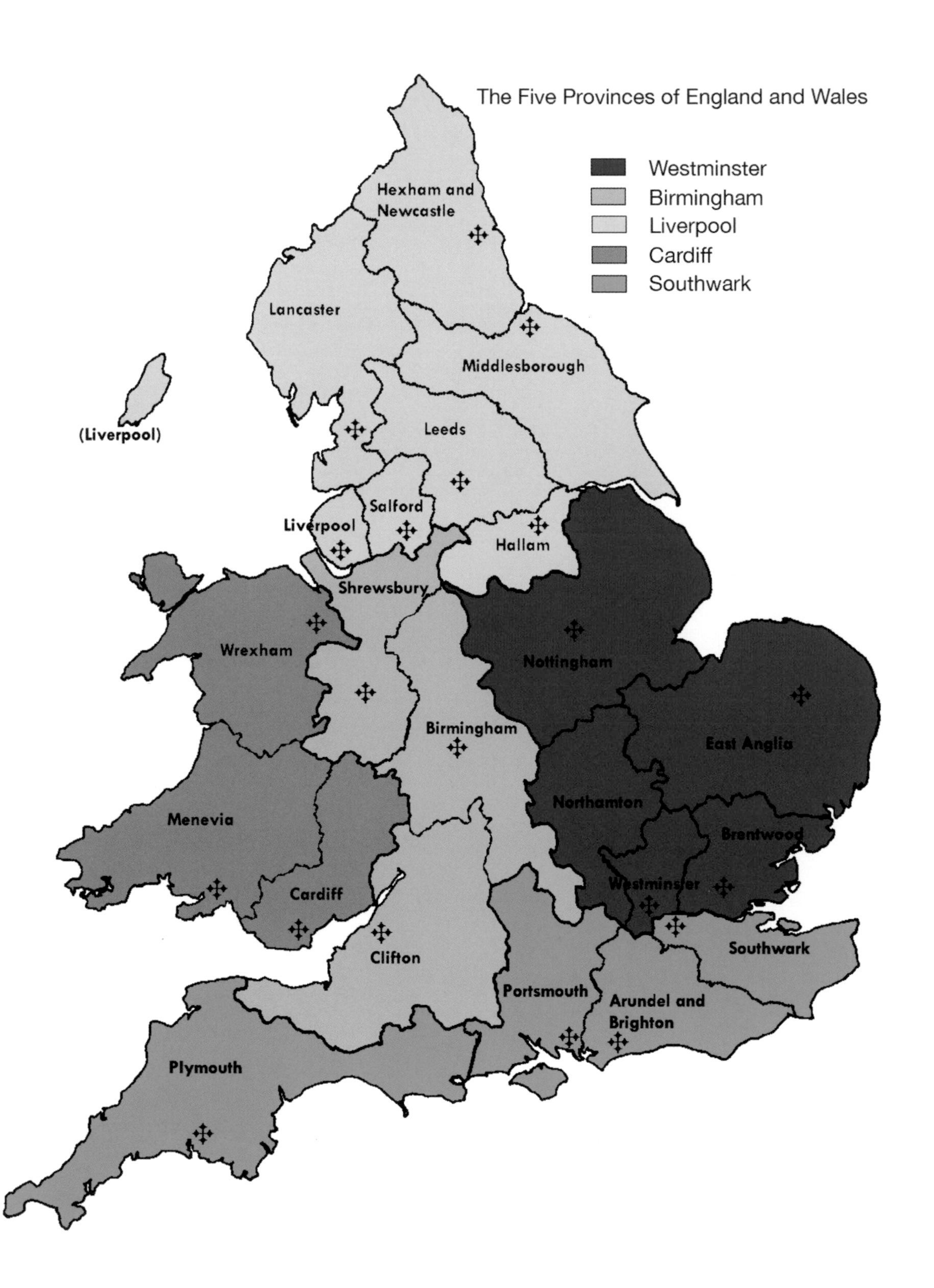
The Five Provinces of England and Wales
Westminster
Birmingham
Liverpool
Cardiff
Southwark
Hexham and Newcastle
Lancaster
Middlesborough
(Liverpool)
Leeds
Salford
Liverpool
Hallam
Shrewsbury
Wrexham
Nottingham
East Anglia
Birmingham
Northamton
Menevia
Brentwood
Westminster
Cardiff
Southwark
Clifton
Portsmouth
Arundel and Brighton
Plymouth

THE UNIVERSAL CHURCH

THE POPE

The Pope is the Bishop of Rome. He is the leader of the Catholic Church throughout the world.

Like every bishop his ministry is to preach the Gospel, teach the people and live a life of service to all. However, the specific ministry of the Pope is to unite the Catholic Church throughout the world.

The Pope is the successor of St. Peter. St. Peter was chosen by Jesus to lead the apostles and the church.

Find Out

How many Catholics are there in the world?

At the heart of St Peter's Basilica, the altar stands over the place venerated as the site of the burial of St Peter whom Jesus called to be shepherd of his Church. Pope Benedict XVI gathers with bishops from around the world to celebrate Mass.

PILGRIMAGE

You will remember that the writer of Genesis expressed God's view of creation in the words 'And God saw that it was good'. That is why the Church calls people to be stewards of creation and to love and respect the world in which we live as a holy place.

All through the history of humankind some places have become special because of the people who lived there and the events that happened there. When people make a special journey to such a holy place it is called a 'pilgrimage'.

Vatican City is an independent state within the city of Rome. In mediaeval times it had its own armies. Nowadays, the Swiss guard are not a fighting force but a security force.

People go on pilgrimage for many different reasons: to walk in the footsteps of Jesus; to pray and reflect on a decision; in search of God; to share life and prayer during the pilgrimage; to be alongside others in their needs.

ROME

Many Catholics go on pilgrimage to Rome. They come to visit St. Peter's Basilica where, according to tradition, St. Peter is buried. St Peter's is in the Vatican City. The city takes its name from the Vatican, the home of the Pope.

Above: View across Rome from the roof of St Peter's Basilica

THE HOLY LAND

Christians call the place where Jesus lived, died and rose from the dead the Holy Land.

BETHLEHEM

The little town where Jesus was born is larger today and in recent years has been the scene of fighting between Israelis and Palestinians.

The Church of the Nativity is built over the cave which has been visited for centuries as the birthplace of Jesus and where his coming into the world is marked by a star.

NAZARETH

The Basilica of the Annunciation marks the world-changing event of Mary's response to God's call.

Mother with her children in Nazareth today

JERUSALEM

The medieval walls of Jerusalem are still a thrilling sight for pilgrims from all over the world.

For Jewish people, the remains of the walls of Solomon's temple are a holy place for prayer.

For Christians, the site of Calvary where Jesus died and rose again is a sacred place.

For Muslims, the Dome of the Rock is one place of pilgrimage.

LOURDES

Lourdes is a town in South-Western France.

Catholics believe that Mary appeared here to St. Bernadette in 1858.

Today, Lourdes is known throughout the world as a special place of pilgrimage for the sick.

PILGRIMS ROUND THE WORLD

Many countries have their own special holy places of Christian pilgimage.

Research

Here are some other places of Christian pilgrimage.

St Francis in Assisi, Italy

St Therese of Lisieux, France

St Padre Pio, San Giovanni Rotondo in the south of Italy

St James, Compostella, Spain

SHRINES OF OUR LADY

at Walsingham in England

at Cardigan in Wales

at Guadalupe in Mexico

at Czestochowa in Poland

at Lourdes in France

at Fatima in Portugal

What can you find out about some of them? You may be able to add to this list by talking with members of your family and friends.

The Communion of Saints

'Communion of Saints' is the collective name given to all members of the Church community whether living or dead. Some members of the Church family are named as martyrs or saints.

Saints are people who have lived in God's way. They show us what God is like – loving, faithful, forgiving, caring for others and God's world.

Some people are 'canonised' which means that the Church recognises and names them as Saints, but everyone who has died and has gone home to God is a saint known only to God.

Collection of icons. In the Orthodox church an icon is seen as a 'window to heaven'. A saint can be a 'window' showing what it means to live God's way.

LIVING GOD'S WAY

Martyrs are people who have been put to death because of their faith. In England and Wales there is a special feast day for men and women who were put to death nearly 500 years ago for their Catholic faith.

The Forty Martyr-Saints of England and Wales.

Top:
St Anthony of Padua

Centre:
St Therese of Lisieux

Below:
St Francis of Assisi

One Father, One Family

Christians cannot pray to God as Father, unless they treat everyone as brothers and sisters, members of one family, created by God to be like God.

St John, one of the apostles, lived to be a very old man. He had a long time to think about all that Jesus had said and done. He wrote letters to people to tell them what he thought was Jesus' most important message. This is what he wrote:

Just think about what great love
God the Father has for us
God calls us his children.
And that is what we are!
My dear friends, we are already
God's children.
And we know that when we
see God,
We will be like God.
We will see God as God really is.
Because we know this,
We try to be loving and kind,
as God is.
Because we are close to God,
We keep away from all that is wrong.

See God's Story 3 p.149
1John 3:1-3

You can read more about some of the English Martyrs and other saints in More Friends of Jesus by Victoria Hummell ra. (McCrimmons 2003)

THE CHURCH'S SACRAMENTS

We know that God is always with us because we see signs of God's love all around the world and in our lives.

There are moments when God's love and presence touch our lives in a special way. The Church's seven sacraments celebrate some of these important moments:

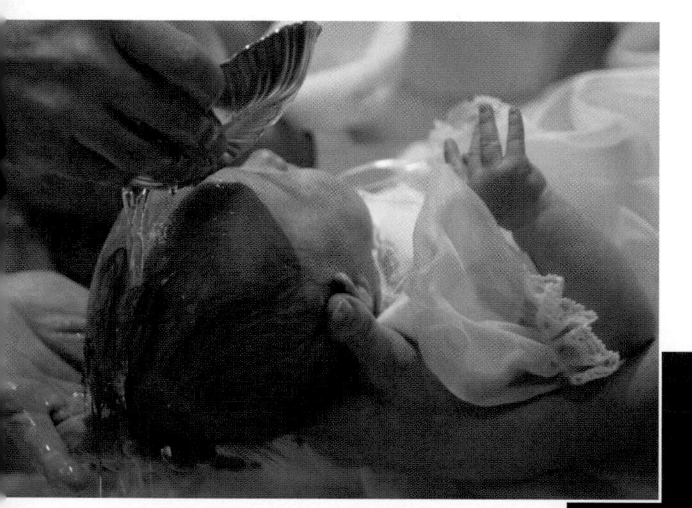

Baptism

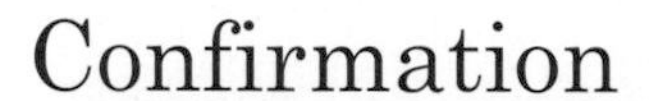

Confirmation

Eucharist

In the celebration of a sacrament we meet God the Father, Son and Holy Spirit.

We celebrate with actions, words, signs and symbols.

The seven sacraments help us to appreciate who God is, what God is like and what God is doing everywhere and for each person. It is God saying 'Here I Am. I am with you and I love you'.

Anointing of the Sick

Reconciliation

Marriage

Holy Orders

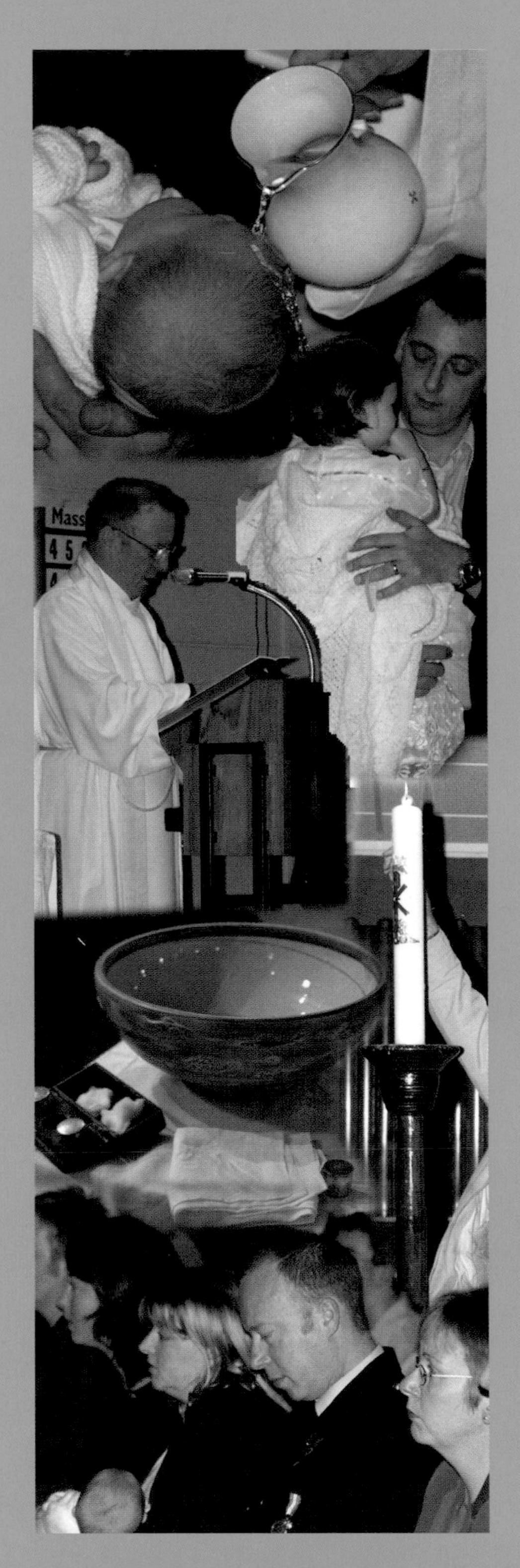

Baptism

WHAT WILL YOU SEE?

oils

water

font

white garment

candle

WHAT WILL YOU HEAR?

questions

readings

prayers

promises

words of Baptism

blessings

WHO WILL BE THERE?

person to be baptised

priest

family and friends

godparents

parish family

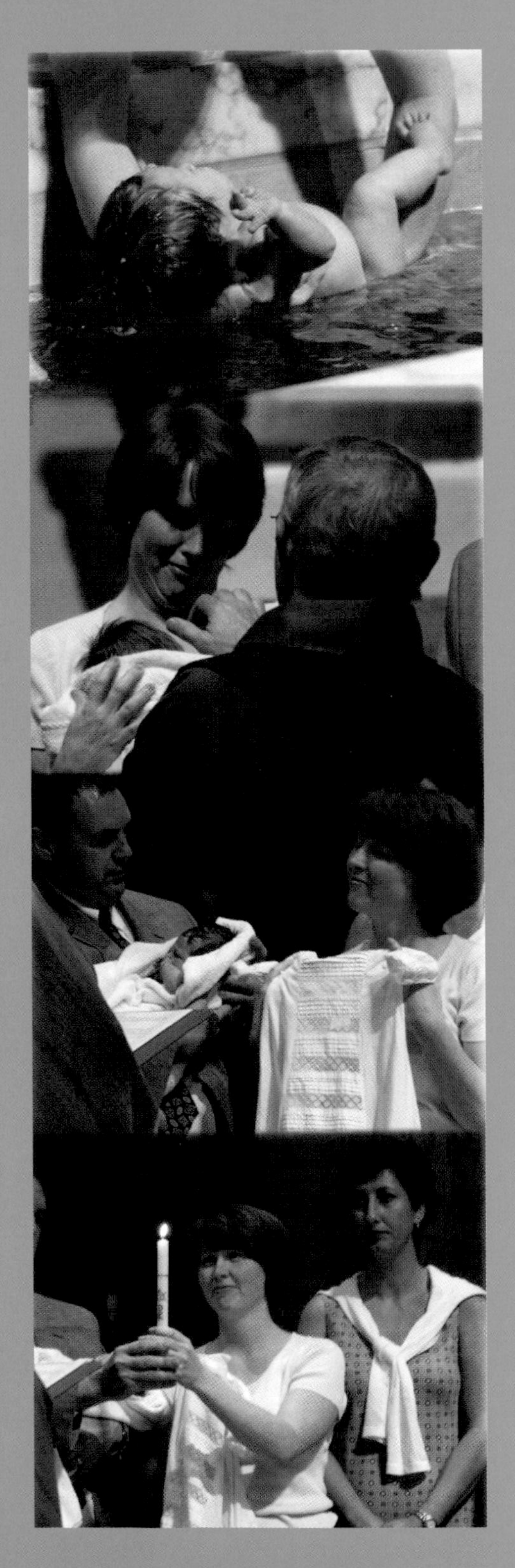

WHAT WILL BE HAPPENING?

welcome

questioning

signing of the cross

listening to God's Word

responding

anointing

pouring of water

anointing with Chrism Oil

clothing with a white garment

lighting of candle

receiving the light

BAPTISM

Baptism is an invitation to join the Church family. When a baby or younger child is baptised, the parents accept the invitation on behalf of their child. Older children and adults accept the invitation themselves. Often adults are baptised at Easter.

Baptism is a special time for the person who is to be baptised for their family and friends and the parish community.

Sometimes the sacrament of Baptism is celebrated when the parish family is gathered together for Mass. At other times family and friends come together in church at another time.

Baptismal celebration for a baby

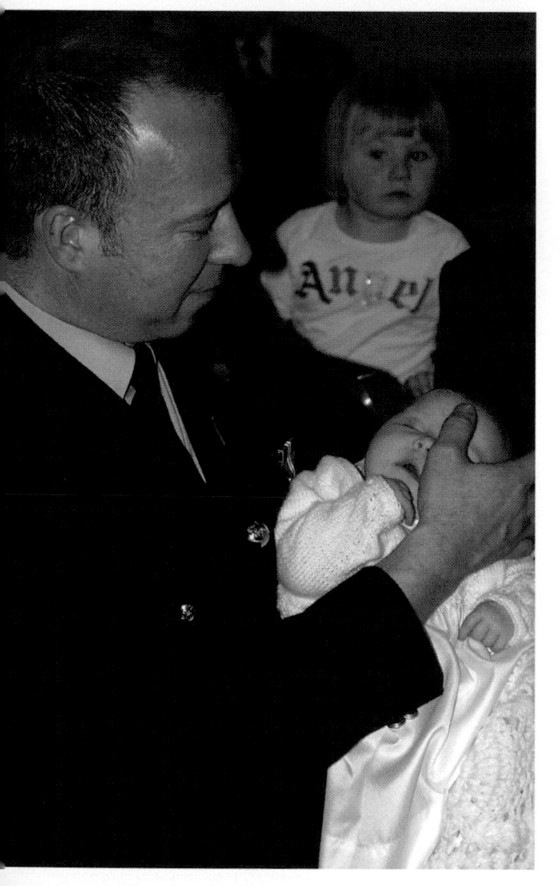

WELCOME

The Easter candle is lit.

The priest greets everyone who has come to the celebration.

He asks the parents, “What name have you given your child?”

When they have answered he asks, “What do you ask of God’s Church for N.....?”

They may reply, “Baptism.”

The priest asks the parents if they will bring up their child to live in God’s way. He asks the godparents if they will help the child’s parents to do this.

THE SIGN OF THE CROSS

Then the priest makes the sign of the cross on the baby’s forehead. Parents and godparents are invited to do the same. This is a sign that the baby is welcomed into the Christian family.

CELEBRATION OF GOD'S WORD

Everyone listens to God's Word in a reading from the Gospel.

Then everyone prays for the baby, his family and everybody present. These prayers are a symbol of care. The priest calls on the saints to 'Pray for us' and will include the patron saint of the church and the saint after whom the baby is named. The prayers ask that this child will be strengthened by God's love and watched over by God at every stage of his life journey.

Then the community respond to God's Word in actions.

ANOINTING

The priest makes the sign of the cross on the baby's chest with the Oil of Catechumens. This oil is a symbol of strength and is one of the oils blessed by the bishop during Holy Week.

CELEBRATION OF THE SACRAMENT

The priest blesses the water which will be used to baptise the baby. Water is a symbol of new life.

The parents and godparents are invited to renew their own baptismal promises as a sign that they will bring up the child in the faith of the Church.

With everyone gathered round the font, the priest pours water over the baby's head, saying, "N, I baptise you in the name of the Father and of the Son, and of the Holy Spirit."

ANOINTING WITH CHRISM

The priest anoints the baby on the crown of the head with the Oil of Chrism. This is a sweet smelling oil mixed with balsam and blessed by the bishop during Holy Week. It is a sign that the baby is to be like Jesus: a priest, to worship God and be holy in God's service, a prophet, to listen to God and help others to hear God's word and a king, ready to serve and care for all the people.

You have become a new creation and clothed yourself in Christ.

As Christ was anointed Priest, Prophet, and King, so may you live always as a member of his body, sharing everlasting life.

THE WHITE GARMENT

A white garment is put on the baby. this is a symbol of becoming a Christian and putting on a new way of life.

THE LIGHTED CANDLE

The priest invites someone from the family to light a candle from the Easter candle saying "Receive the light of Christ." Both candles are symbols of the light of Christ. Jesus is the light. His light is for everyone.

The priest says to the parents and godparents, "This light is entrusted to you to be kept burning brightly. This child of yours has been enlightened by Christ. She is to walk always as a child of the light."

May she keep the flame of faith alive in her heart.

THE OUR FATHER

The priest invites everyone present to welcome the new member of the Church. As a sign of the baby's right to take part in the Eucharist, everyone prays in the words Jesus gave us: "Our Father...

BLESSINGS OF PARENTS AND PEOPLE

The priest blesses the mother and father of the baby and finally the whole community assembled in the church.

Confirmation

WHAT WILL YOU SEE?

Oil of Chrism

Mitre

Crozier

WHAT WILL YOU HEAR?

words of welcome

prayers

readings

promises

words of Confirmation

WHO WILL BE THERE?

candidates for Confirmation

bishop

sponsor

priest

catechist

family and friends

parish family

WHAT WILL BE HAPPENING?

gathering

readings

calling forward

questions

laying on of hands

anointing

receiving the Holy Spirit

CONFIRMATION

Confirmation is also a Sacrament of Initiation. Confirmation strengthens or 'confirms' the baptised person's relationship with God and the Church.

In England and Wales, many people are baptised when they are babies and confirmed when they are older.

The sacrament of Confirmation is celebrated during a parish Mass. It is usually a Bishop who confirms.

A person who chooses to be confirmed promises to live as a Christian and follow the teaching of Jesus with the help of the Holy Spirit. Sometimes people choose a Confirmation name, most often the name of a saint whose example of living God's way they respect.

Celebration of Confirmation

GATHERING

Those to be confirmed, along with their family, friends, sponsors and the parish family gather for a Mass of celebration. The gathering hymn is often a prayer to the Holy Spirit.

The Bishop welcomes everyone. He wears a mitre and carries a crozier, a long staff curved at the top like a shepherd's crook. This symbolises his role of caring for all the people in his diocese as a good shepherd cares for the whole flock.

LITURGY OF THE WORD

The readings from Scripture are chosen to remind all those present of the gifts the Holy Spirit brings to God's Church. They may speak of wisdom, open-mindedness, discipleship, strength, hope and the role of the Holy Spirit to help Christians remember all that Jesus taught.

After the Gospel, the candidates are presented to the Bishop and the gathered community. Each candidate stands when his or her name is called.

The Bishop, in his homily, usually addresses the candidates directly on this important day in their lives. He may remind them of the day of Pentecost when the apostles received the Holy Spirit as Jesus had promised.

After the homily all who have been baptised renew the promises made at Baptism.

CELEBRATION OF THE SACRAMENT

The candidates are called forward together. The bishop, often joined by the priests present, extends his hands over them. He prays that the Holy Spirit will strengthen them with special gifts.

Then they are presented individually to the Bishop by the parish priest and their sponsor. The priest and their sponsors represent the community which has introduced the candidate into the life of faith of the Church.

Each candidate goes to the Bishop. The sponsor places his or her right hand on the candidate's shoulder and gives the candidate's newly chosen name to the Bishop.

Be sealed with the gift of the Holy Spirit.

ANOINTING WITH CHRISM

The Bishop dips his right thumb into the oil of chrism and makes the sign of the cross on the forehead of the candidate saying, "Be sealed with the gift of the Holy Spirit."

He or she responds, "Amen."

The cross is a sign of a follower of Jesus.

ONE BODY

The Bishop says, "Peace be with you."

The newly confirmed reply, "And also with you."

Special prayers follow for those who have been confirmed, their parents, godparents and sponsors, for the Church throughout the world and for the entire human family.

The Mass continues in its usual pattern.

Sometimes the newly confirmed are invited to join the priest around the altar to pray the Our Father as a symbol of the communion with one another and God which is the gift of the Holy Spirit.

Peace be with you

EUCHARIST

WHAT WILL YOU SEE?

altar

host

chalice

ciborium

WHO WILL BE THERE?

parish family

friends

priest

servers

readers

Special Ministers of Holy Communion

WHAT WILL YOU HEAR?

singing

prayers

the readings

homily

Prayers of the Faithful

Eucharistic prayer

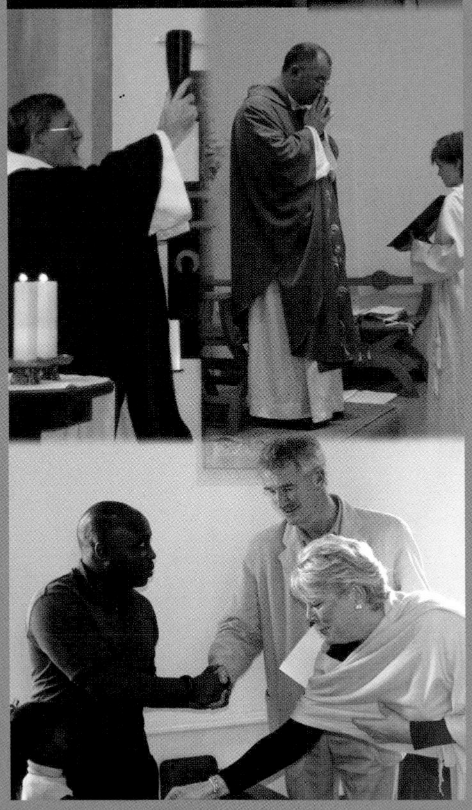

WHAT WILL BE HAPPENING?

gathering

entrance procession

gospel procession

presentation of the gifts

consecration of bread
and wine

presenting consecrated host

presenting the chalice of
consecrated wine

exchanging the sign of peace

receiving communion

quiet prayer

blessing

sending out

Eucharist

The Church family gathers together to share in the sacrament of the Eucharist.

Eucharist means thanksgiving. With Christ the Church comes to give thanks to God. The Eucharist remembers and celebrates the life, death, and resurrection of Jesus.

At communion people receive Jesus in Holy Communion.

The sacrament of the Eucharist brings us closer to Jesus and to one another. The sacrament of the Eucharist is a sacrament that people receive often.

First Holy Communion is a time of celebration for the parish family.

Usually communion is distributed at every Mass. Sometimes a Special Minister of Holy Communion will lead a service of the Word with Holy Communion if there is no priest to celebrate Mass.

The priest or Eucharistic ministers will take communion to members of the parish family who cannot get to church, such as the sick and the house bound.

GATHERING

Outside a church on Sunday people of different ages and different races are arriving in cars, on foot, perhaps off a bus.

Inside the church, the welcomers greet people and offer them hymn books or mass books. Other people will be preparing everything for the celebration: candles, water and wine, hosts, books for the readers and the priests. The musicians will be tuning up or running through a piece of music.

In the sacristy the altar servers will be gathering and the priest and deacon will be putting on their vestments.

When everything is ready they all sing the Gathering Song and the procession of altar servers, readers, deacon and priest enters the church.

The priest and deacon kiss the altar because it is the symbol of Jesus and it is with Jesus and by the power of the Holy Spirit that the Church offers this Eucharist to God the Father.

The first words the priest says remind everyone of this: In the name of the Father and of the Son and of the Holy Spirit. The priest says "The Lord be with you".

The congregation replies "And also with you."

PENITENTIAL RITE

The Eucharist is the Church's thanksgiving for the life, death and resurrection of Jesus. It is the sacrament of God's love, mercy and forgiveness. So the priest invites the people to call to mind our need for God's mercy and forgiveness.

After a moment of silence he may say:

You were sent to heal the contrite: Lord, have mercy
Congregation: Lord have mercy
You came to call sinners: Christ have mercy.
Congregation: Christ, have mercy
You plead for us at the right hand of the Father:
Lord, have mercy.
Congregation: Lord, have mercy.
The priest says: May Almighty God have mercy on us, forgive us our sins and bring us to everlasting life.
Congregation: Amen

GLORY TO GOD

The response to God's mercy and forgiveness is a song of praise: Glory to God. The first words echo the heavenly message to the shepherds when Jesus was born: Glory to God in the highest and peace to his people on earth.

The priest then prays the opening prayer for that Sunday and everyone sits down for the Liturgy of the Word.

LITURGY OF THE WORD

The readings proclaim the message of God's love and truth, mercy and forgiveness as it has been told by the People of God in the Old and the New Testament.

On Sunday there are three readings. The first reading is usually from the Old Testament. It is followed by a responsorial psalm. The people say or sing the response to each verse. The second reading is usually from one of the letters in the New Testament.

At the end each reader says:
This is the Word of the Lord.

The people respond: Thanks be to God.

Then the altar servers and the deacon or priest prepare for the gospel reading. The deacon or priest and two altar servers with lighted candles go to the ambo. In some churches the deacon or priest will hold up and carry the Book of the Gospels to the ambo.

The people greet the gospel by singing or saying 'Alleluia' which means 'Praise God!'.

The deacon or priest says:

"A reading from the holy gospel according to ..."

He makes the sign of the cross on the Book of the Gospels, on his forehead, lips and heart.

The people make the sign of the cross on their foreheads, lips and hearts.

At the end the deacon or priest says: This is the Gospel of the Lord.

The people respond: Praise to you, Lord Jesus Christ.

Everyone sits down to listen to the homily. The priest will talk about the readings to help people to understand them and think about how they are living in God's way.

After the homily everyone prays the Creed, expressing their faith.

This part of the liturgy ends with the Prayers of the Faithful. These ask God's love and mercy for the Church and the World.

Liturgy of the Word with Children

In some parishes children have their own Liturgy of the Word. The priest gives them a children's bible and they go out with the catechists. They come back in time to join in the presentation of the gifts.

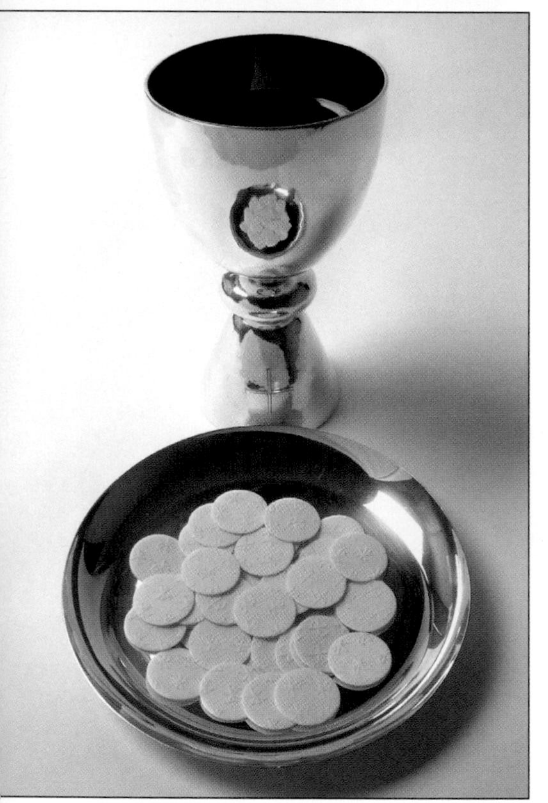

LITURGY OF THE EUCHARIST: PREPARATION OF THE GIFTS

Before Mass begins, bread and wine are placed on a table at the back of the church. Now members of the parish family carry the bread and wine up to the altar. The collection is taken and brought up to the altar with the gifts.

Offering the bread the priest prays:

"Blessed are you Lord God of all creation. Through your goodness we have this bread to offer, which earth has given and human hands have made. It will become for us the bread of life."

Everyone responds, "Blessed be God for ever."

Offering the wine the priest prays:

"Blessed are you Lord God of all creation. Through your goodness we have this wine to offer, fruit of the vine and work of human hands. It will become our spiritual drink."

Everyone responds, "Blessed be God for ever."

Sometimes at Mass incense is used. Incense is a symbol of holiness. One of the gifts of the wise men at Christmas was frankincense, symbolising the holy child.

The priest incenses the altar and the gifts of bread and wine that will be made holy and become Jesus, the holy one.

EUCHARISTIC PRAYER

The Eucharistic Prayer gives thanks for all God's goodness. The greatest of all gifts is Jesus and in this prayer the Church remembers the special meal of the Last Supper.

Holding the host the priest says,

"Take this, all of you and eat it:

this is my body, which will be given up for you."

Holding the chalice the priest says,

"When supper was ended, he took the cup. Again he gave you thanks and praise, gave the cup to his disciples, and said:

"Take this all of you and drink from it: this is the cup of my blood, the blood of the new and everlasting covenant. It will be shed for you and for all so that sins may be forgiven. Do this in memory of me."

The priest says,
"Let us proclaim the mystery of faith."

Everyone joins in the acclamation.

Christ has died,

Christ is risen,

Christ will come again.

'AMEN'

The Eucharistic Prayer ends with words of faith in God the Father, Son and Holy Spirit.

The priest says,

"Through him,

with him,

in him,

in the unity of the Holy Spirit,

all glory and honour is yours,

almighty Father

for ever and ever."

The people say or sing: "Amen."

'Amen' is a Hebrew word. It means 'Let it be so', 'we agree'.

The Mystery of Faith

A 'mystery of faith' is something that is beyond human power to explain. The Church believes that Jesus is truly present because of what he said.

His words about the bread and wine are Jesus saying to us 'This is my living presence, this is myself, it is me'.

Other Acclamations used are:

Dying you destroyed our death
rising you restored our life,
Lord Jesus, come in glory.

When we eat this bread and drink this cup,
we proclaim your death, Lord Jesus, until you come in glory.

Lord, by your cross and resurrection
you have set us free.
You are the Saviour of the world.

COMMUNION RITE

The Christian family comes to the Lord's table united in love of Jesus and one another. Communion with Jesus is celebrated in prayers and actions.

First everyone prays the Our Father, the prayer that Jesus gave his friends.

Sometimes the priest will invite the children to gather around the altar.

Sometimes people join hands as they pray.

Then the priest prays for peace and invites everyone to share a Sign of Peace. People say to one another 'Peace be with you', 'The peace of Christ' or just 'Peace'.

Everyone prays or sings the prayer 'Lamb of God'.

The priest invites people to come to communion. He holds up the sacred host and the chalice and says,
"This is the Lamb of God who takes away the sins of the world. Happy are those who are called to his supper."
The congregation responds. "Lord I am not worthy to receive you, but only say the word and I shall be healed."

The priest receives the Body and Blood of Christ and gives communion to the Special Ministers of Holy Communion and servers. Then the people come in procession to receive Jesus.

Prayer for peace and unity

Lord, Jesus Christ, you said to your apostles: I leave you peace, my peace I give you. Look not on our sins, but on the faith of your Church, and grant us the peace and unity of your kingdom where you live for ever and ever. Amen.

The priest or the special ministers hold up the host to each person saying. “The Body of Christ.” They do the same with the chalice saying, “The Blood of Christ.” Each time the person responds, “Amen.”

People who do not receive communion receive a blessing.

Sometimes this is the time when Special Ministers of Holy Communion go out to take communion to those who are sick or housebound.

The priest says a final prayer of thanksgiving.

SENDING FORTH

If there are any announcements about parish life they are made now.

The priest prays a final blessing. Then he says, “Go in the peace of Christ” or “The Mass is ended, go in peace” or “Go in peace to love and serve the Lord.” It is a reminder that everyone is called to live the communion they have celebrated every day and in every place.

Everyone responds, “Thanks be to God.”

Reconciliation

WHO WILL BE THERE?

priest

penitent

members of the parish family

WHAT WILL YOU SEE?

a place to meet the priest

a crucifix

hands raised in blessing

WHAT WILL YOU HEAR?

words of welcome

readings

prayers of sorrow

words of absolution

WHAT WILL BE HAPPENING?

liturgy of the word

examination of conscience

confession of sins

penance

absolution and forgiveness

Reconciliation

In the sacrament of Reconciliation we celebrate God's love and mercy. We learn about the joys and challenges of living as a follower of Jesus in love and peace.

During Reconciliation the Church celebrates the love and mercy of God and calls people to confess sins, seek forgiveness and be reconciled to God and to one another.

Reconciliation is known by various names: Penance, Confession, Sacrament of Forgiveness.

It is another sacrament we can celebrate often. It helps us to live as followers of Jesus.

Sometimes the parish family comes together to celebrate a Service of Reconciliation. During this time individuals may make their confession to a priest. At other times the priest and one member of the parish family celebrate the sacrament.

Before confessing their sins people will have spent some time thinking about ways in which they have not lived as Jesus did. This is called an examination of conscience.

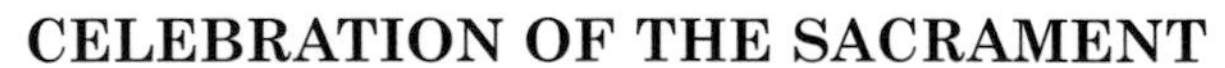

CELEBRATION OF THE SACRAMENT

At the sacrament of Reconciliation the priest welcomes the person in the name of Jesus. They make the Sign of the Cross together. Sometimes they listen to a passage from the Bible.

The person confesses his or her sins to the priest.

The priest asks them to say or do something to make up for their sins and as a sign that they will try to do better in the future. This is called a penance.

The person prays an act of sorrow, such as:

"O my God, because you are so good, I am very sorry that I have sinned against you and with the help of your grace I will not sin again."

The promise to make a new start is called a firm purpose of amendment.

The priest then raises his hand over the person and says the words of forgiveness and absolution.

"I absolve you from your sins in the name of the Father, and of the Son, and of the Holy Spirit. Amen."

Together they say a prayer for God's forgiveness and love.

Anointing of the Sick

WHAT WILL YOU SEE?

olive oil

priest

person being anointed

WHO WILL BE THERE?

sick person

priest

family/friends

parish community

WHAT WILL BE HAPPENING?

laying on of hands

anointing with oil

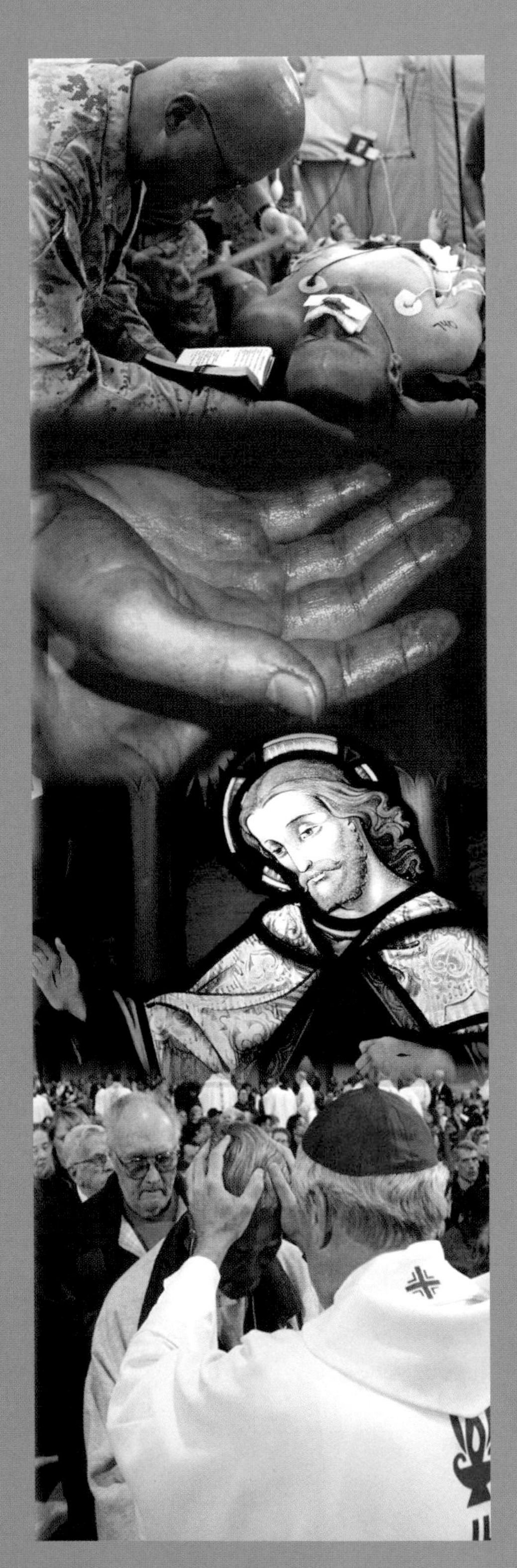

WHAT WILL YOU HEAR?

words of welcome

readings

litany

prayers of blessing

prayer of anointing

Give life and health to our brothers and sisters on whom we lay our hands in your name.

Through this anointing may the Lord in his love and mercy help you with the grace of the Holy Spirit. Amen!

SACRAMENT OF ANOINTING OF THE SICK

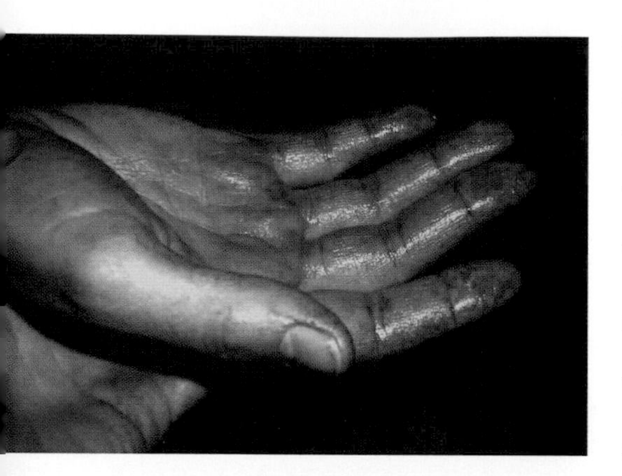

The sacrament of the Anointing of the Sick celebrates God's gifts of hope, strength and healing, life and friendship with God the Father, with Jesus and with one another.

The celebration uses:

actions – anointing

words – prayers

and symbols – oil, sign of the cross.

CELEBRATION OF THE SACRAMENT WITHIN MASS

Sometimes the celebration takes place within a Mass for all sick people and their families and friends. Often the celebration is for one sick person in hospital or at home.

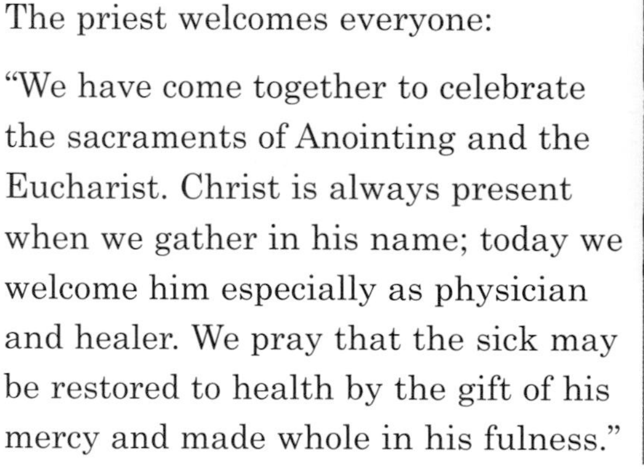

The priest welcomes everyone:

"We have come together to celebrate the sacraments of Anointing and the Eucharist. Christ is always present when we gather in his name; today we welcome him especially as physician and healer. We pray that the sick may be restored to health by the gift of his mercy and made whole in his fulness."

LITANY

After the Liturgy of the Word there is a special prayer called a litany.

Let us pray to God for our brothers and sisters and for all those who devote themselves to caring for them.
Bless N. and N. and fill them with new hope and strength: Lord have mercy.
Response: Lord have mercy.
Relieve their pain: Lord have mercy.
Response: Lord have mercy.
Sustain all the sick with your power:
Lord have mercy.
Response: Lord have mercy.
Assist all who care for the sick:
Lord have mercy.
Response: Lord have mercy.
Give life and health to our brothers and sisters on whom we lay our hands in your name: Lord have mercy.
Response: Lord have mercy.

ANOINTING

The priest lays his hands on the head of each sick person. He anoints the forehead of each sick person saying:
"Through this anointing may the Lord in his love and mercy help you with the grace of the Holy Spirit. Amen."
He anoints the hands of each sick person saying,
"May the Lord who frees you from sin save you and raise you up. Amen."

FINAL PRAYER FOR ALL THOSE WHO ARE SICK

Father in heaven,
through this holy anointing
grant our brothers and sisters
comfort in their suffering.
When they are afraid,
give them courage,
when afflicted, give them patience,
when dejected, afford them hope,
and when alone,
assure them of the support
of your holy people.
We ask this through Christ our Lord.
Response: Amen

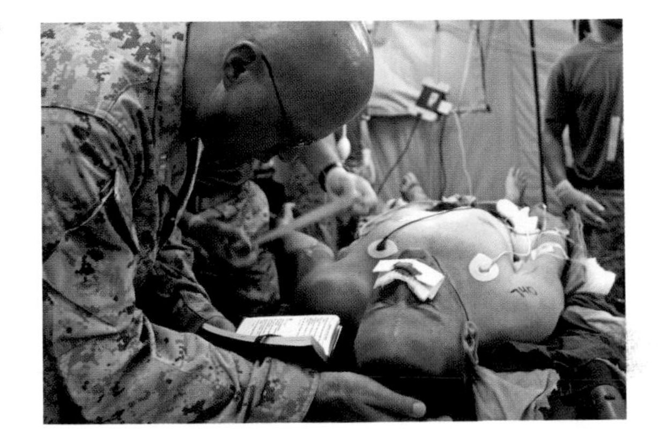

Marriage

WHAT WILL YOU SEE?

rings

flowers

WHAT WILL YOU HEAR?

music

prayers

scripture readings

promises

blessings

WHO WILL BE THERE?

community of family and friends of the bride and groom

priest or deacon

witnesses

registrar

WHAT WILL BE HAPPENING?

gathering

welcome

joining hands

giving and receiving of rings

signing of register

SACRAMENT OF MARRIAGE

Marriage is a sacrament which celebrates the gift of love and life and friendship with God the Father, with Jesus and with one another. A man and woman choose to be married in church because Jesus is important in their lives. This is their response to God's call to live a life filled with love for one another.

The family and friends of the bride and groom gather to celebrate this sacrament with them.

It is a very special occasion as, usually, people receive this sacrament only once.

Another name for the sacrament is Matrimony. The celebration is called a wedding.

Sometimes the celebration takes place during a Mass. At other times it is a separate liturgy.

CELEBRATION OF THE SACRAMENT WITHIN MASS

When two people get married in church they are professing their faith that God is with them. They are asking God to bless them. Their family, friends and sometimes members of the parish community are present with them and praying for them.

The family and friends of the bride and groom gather in church. When the bride arrives everyone stands to welcome her and joyful music is played.

After the prayers of welcome and the Scripture readings, the priest calls the bride and groom to stand in front of the altar. He asks them if they are freely choosing to enter into marriage with each other.

PROMISES

After each has said, 'I will', they make special marriage promises to one another.

The man and woman join hands as each promises:

I call upon these persons here present,

to witness that I, (name)...

do take thee, (name)...

to be my lawful wedded (wife/husband)

to have and to hold

from this day forward,

for better, for worse,

for richer, for poorer,

in sickness and in health,

to love and to cherish,

till death do us part.

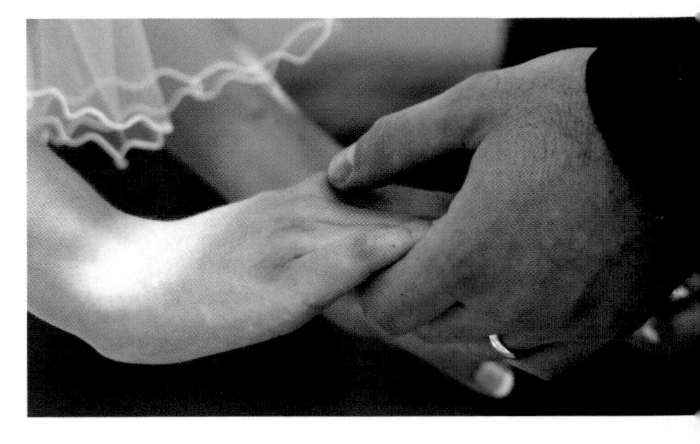

BLESSING AND GIVING OF RINGS

The priest prays:

May the Lord bless these rings
which you give to each other,
as the sign of your love and fidelity
The bride and groom say to each other
"N, take this ring as a sign of my love and fidelity. In the name of the Father, and of the Son, and of the Holy Spirit."

SIGNING THE REGISTER

The newly married couple sign a special register of marriages and two witnesses sign with them. This action is done with the Registrar of Marriages.

NUPTIAL BLESSING

After the Our Father the priest prays the nuptial blessing which ends with these words:

Father,

keep them always true to your commandments.

Keep them faithful in marriage

and let them be examples of Christian life.

Give them the strength which comes from the Gospel

so that they may be witnesses of Christ to others.

Bless them with children

and help them to be good parents.

May they live to see their children's children.

And after a happy old age,

grant them fullness of life with the saints

in the kingdom of heaven.

We ask this through Christ our Lord.

Everyone responds, "Amen."

The husband and wife leave the church together to joyful music, followed by their family and friends.

Ordination

WHAT WILL YOU SEE?

stole

chasuble

oil

paten

chalice

WHAT WILL YOU HEAR?

music

prayers

scripture readings

promises

blessings

WHO WILL BE THERE?

family and friends

parish community

priest

bishop

deacons

ordinands

WHAT WILL BE HAPPENING?

gathering

welcome

laying on of hands

anointing with oil

clothing with vestments

presentation of paten and chalice

sign of peace

SACRAMENT OF ORDINATION

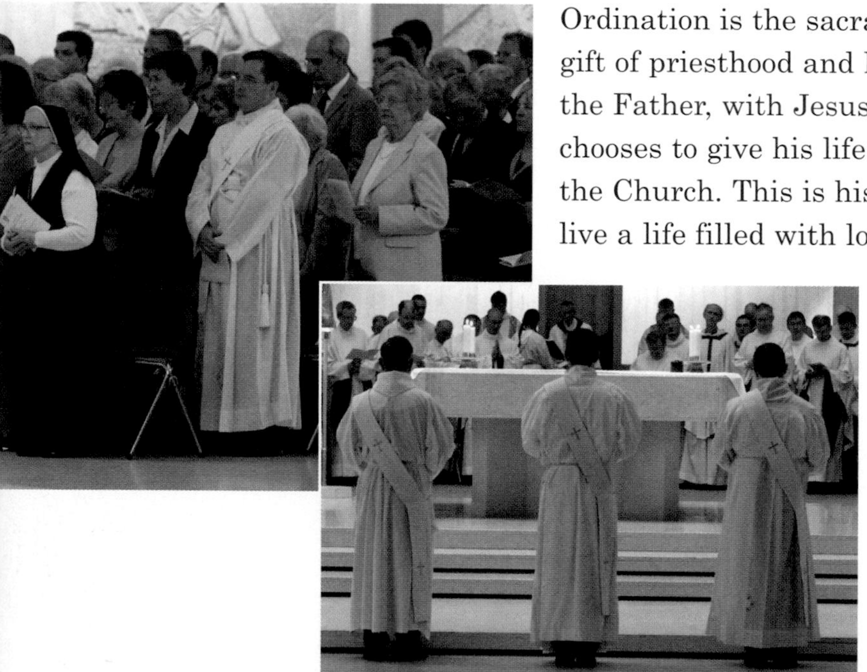

Ordination is the sacrament which celebrates the gift of priesthood and life and friendship with God the Father, with Jesus and one another. A priest chooses to give his life for the service of others in the Church. This is his response to God's call to live a life filled with love for God's people.

Another name for ordination is the Sacrament of Holy Orders. There are three Holy Orders: for deacons, priests and bishops.

This sacrament is celebrated during Mass. It is the Bishop who ordains.

CELEBRATION OF THE SACRAMENT

The family and friends of the ordinand, the person who is to be ordained, gather for the celebration.

The Bishop, priests, deacons and ordinand process to the altar and the Mass begins.

The ordinand is called forward from the congregation. The ordinand stands in front of the Bishop. The Bishop asks him if he is freely choosing to be ordained and will promise to be a good and faithful priest and he answers, " I am, with the help of God."

The bishop kneels and with the congregation prays the Litany of the Saints, during this the ordinand lies prostrate.

LAYING ON OF HANDS

The Bishop lays his hands on his head. The priests present also lay hands on the head of the ordinand. The Bishop prays the prayer of consecration:

"Almighty Father,

grant to this servant of yours the dignity of priesthood.

Renew within him the spirit of holiness.

As a co-worker with the order of bishops

may he be faithful to the ministry that he receives from you, Lord God,

and be to others a model of right conduct."

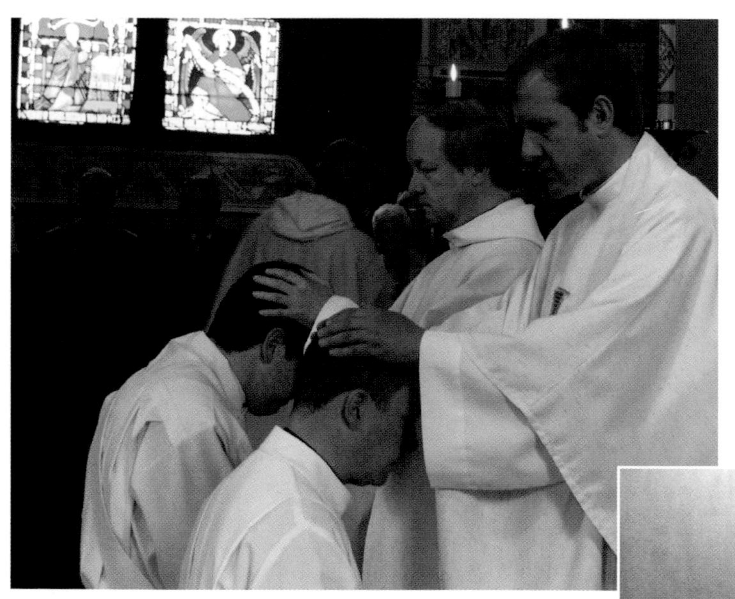

RECEIVING STOLE AND CHASUBLE

The newly ordained priest then receives his stole and chasuble. A stole is worn as a sign of service and priesthood. A chasuble is a loose, coloured top vestment worn for the celebration of Mass.

ANOINTING

The bishop anoints the priest's hands with oil of chrism as a sign of consecration. This means he has promised to spend his life in service for others.

RECEIVING PATEN AND CHALICE

The newly ordained priest receives from the bishop a paten with a host upon it and a chalice with wine in it. The bishop says, "Accept from the holy people of God the gifts to be offered to him."

KISS OF PEACE

The bishop gives the new priest the kiss of peace. The other priests also greet him, welcoming and congratulating him with a kiss of peace.

CHRISTIAN LIVING

All through the year the Church family celebrates Jesus. The seasons and feasts are an annual journey through the life, death and resurrection of Jesus.

There is also a cycle of feasts of saints to celebrate. In these pages you will discover the signs and symbols of these seasons and feasts.

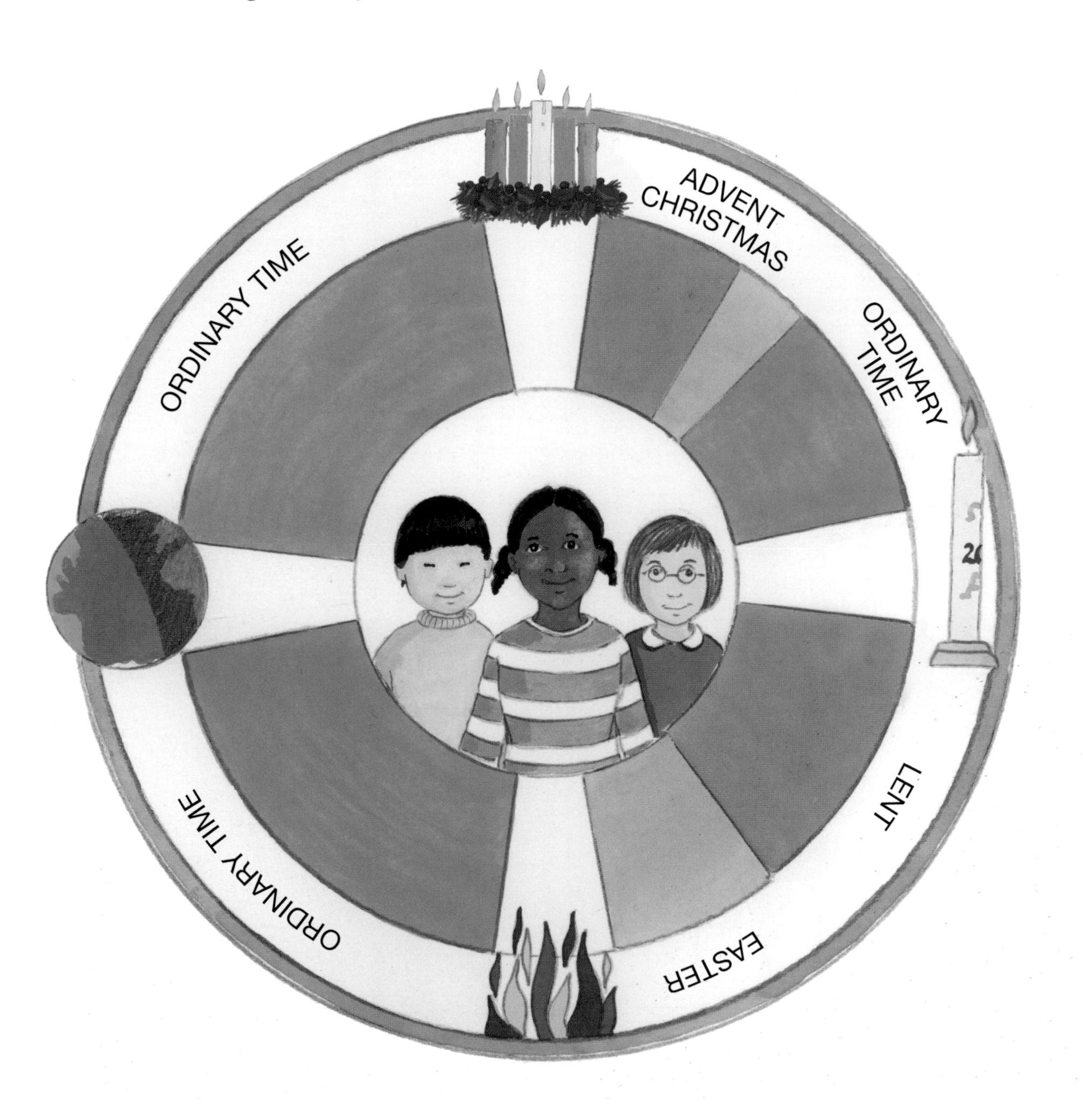

ADVENT

Advent marks the beginning of the Church's year. The word ADVENT comes from the Latin word 'adventus' which means 'a drawing near'. The event that is drawing near is Christmas, the celebration of the birth of Jesus. The four Sundays before Christmas Day are known as the four Sundays of Advent. This is a time of waiting in joyful hope for the coming of Jesus into the world.

The symbols, prayers and readings of the season help us to reflect on God's love which is made known in the the wonderful gift of Jesus.

ADVENT SYMBOLS

Each Sunday one candle is lit on the **Advent Wreath** to mark the time of waiting for Christ's birthday.

The purple candles are a sign that this is a penitential season, when people make an extra effort to be more faithful in prayer and more loving by doing something practical for others, especially those in need.

Prayer of blessing for the Advent wreath

Dear God,
we thank you for giving us Jesus
to be the light in our darkness.
Bless us as we gather in his name
and bless this wreath as a sign of his light among us.
We ask this blessing through
Jesus our Lord. Amen.
(Adapted from A Book of Blessings, Canadian Conference of Catholic Bishops)

The pink candle is a sign that the penitential time is joyful too, because the coming of Jesus brings joy to all people.

The white candle is a symbol of Jesus whose coming brings light in the darkness of wintertime.

The **Advent Calendar** at home and at school is a countdown to Christmas. Christian calendars will often have suggestions about things to do to show love and care for others.

Pictures on the right from top to bottom: Moses, John the Baptist and Our Lady taken from a homemade Advent Calendar.

Advent People

Each candle on the Advent wreath represents an important aspect of waiting.

There were long centuries of waiting for the people of Israel.

Isaiah was an important prophet who was born about 765 years before Jesus. He was a skillful poet. The Church's Advent readings from Isaiah look forward joyfully to the coming of the Promised One, the Messiah whom God would send and who would bring peace and justice on earth.

When the Messiah comes:

'The blind will be able to see and the deaf will be able to hear.
Those who are lame will leap and dance.
Those who are dumb will shout for joy.
Everyone will sing and shout for gladness
Everlasting joy will be seen on their faces.
They will be happy for ever, free from all sorrow and sadness.'

(Isaiah 35: 9-10; God's Story 3 p.61)

From the Book of the Prophet Isaiah

Go up to the top of a high mountain,
joyful messenger to my people.
Shout as loud as you can.
Proclaim the good news for everyone to hear.
Say to them all, "Here is your God."
Your God is coming strong, powerful, true and dependable.
Your God is coming like a shepherd feeding his flock, gathering the lambs, holding them close.
Yes, God is coming like a shepherd looking after the mother ewes,
leading them to a place where they can rest.

(based on Isaiah 40:9-11) God's Story 3 p.62

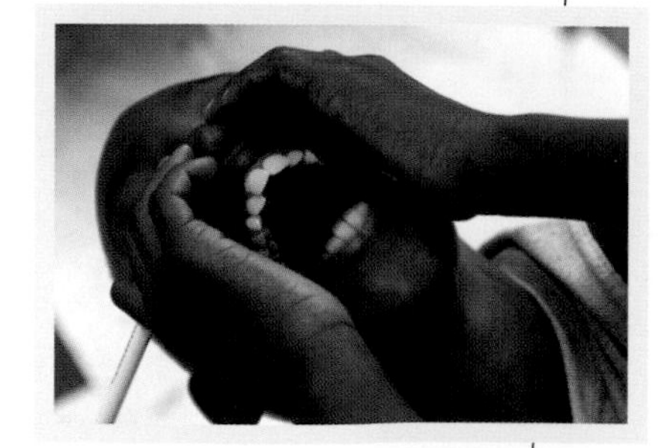

At the time when Isaiah was encouraging the people by teaching them to look forward to the coming of the Messiah, the people of Judah were conquered and they had almost lost heart, fearing that the Saviour would never come.

Isaiah used the idea of the return of the victorious hero as he painted a word-picture for the people to show them what they must do to prepare for the coming of the Messiah. They must prepare a way right across the desert, a straight road right across the wastelands, fill in the valleys and level the mountains, take the top of each hill and turn it into a plateau and even lower the cliffs. Then they would be able to see God coming from the very far distance, coming in glory, for everyone to see.

From the Book of the Prophet Isaiah

A voice cries out

"Prepare, a way for our God

in the wilderness.

Make a straight path across the desert.

Let every valley be filled in.

Let every mountain and hill be levelled.

Then the glory of God will be made known,

and the whole human race will see it."

(based on Isaiah 40:3-5)

You can read the story of the birth of John the Baptist in God's Story 3 p70 and p73.

More Advent People

John the Baptist was the one who would prepare the way for Jesus. He would get people ready to listen to what Jesus had to say.

Hundreds of years after Isaiah, Mark's Gospel began with the story of John the Baptist, preparing the people for the coming of the Messiah. Mark says that John is the 'voice in the wilderness' that Isaiah was talking about. The people John the Baptist was speaking to were excited. They knew that the prophets, over hundreds of years, had told people of God's promise. They thought John might be the one they were waiting for, the Christ.

But John said, "I baptise you with water, but someone is coming who is more powerful than I am, and I am not fit to undo the strap of his sandals." (Luke 3:15-16)

Mary

From the beginning of time, God had been preparing the world for the coming of Jesus. When the time came, God chose the one who was to be his mother. God did not choose someone because she was important, rich or clever. God looks at the heart. Mary loved God very much. All the people around her did not know this. They thought she was a very ordinary young girl who did all the ordinary things – cooking, cleaning, making clothes, washing-up and having fun with her friends.

But God prepared Mary in a very special way to be the mother of Jesus. Every day she tried to please God in ordinary ways as she grew to be a young woman.

Mary was betrothed, or engaged, to a man named Joseph who, though he was a carpenter, belonged to the family of the great King David who had lived a thousand years before this time. Before they were married God's messenger, Gabriel, visited Mary and announced to her the good news that she was to be the mother of God's Son, Jesus. She heard that her cousin Elizabeth was also expecting a baby. As soon as she heard this news she set out to visit Elizabeth to share her joy in the birth of her son, John. This was the same John who became John the Baptist.

Mary prepared for the birth of her son, just like any other mother. Above all, she prepared herself. That is why each year during the season of Advent, the Church family reflects on Mary's story as it prepares to celebrate the birth of Jesus on Christmas Day.

You can read the story of the Annunciation and Visitation in God's Story 3 p71 and p72.

Christmas

Christmas is the season during which the Christian family thinks about and celebrates God's gift of Jesus, the best gift of all.

The Christmas season begins with the celebration of the Vigil Mass on the evening of the 24th December and ends with the celebration of the Baptism of Jesus on the Sunday after the Epiphany.

The Church tells the Christmas story by using symbols, by listening to stories from the Bible which tell about the gift of Jesus, by singing hymns, carols and songs, and by saying special prayers.

If we read the Scripture stories carefully we learn more about God. Matthew and Luke both tell stories about the birth of Jesus and the weeks and months that followed. These stories are very different and each has its own message. Luke tells of the shepherds, very ordinary workmen. Matthew of the magi, important men, well-known for their wisdom. They travel from the East to the land of the Jewish people.

Christmas Symbols

At church, at home and at school there will be a Christmas crib.

The crib is a symbol of the humble and poor situation in which Jesus was born. The figures in the crib tell the Christmas story of Mary and Joseph who travelled to Bethlehem. There Jesus was born and was laid in a manger because there was no room in the inn. There the shepherds came to see the Saviour. They are a sign of all who are poor and marginalised. There the wise men came from the East. They were not Jewish and are a sign that Jesus is for all the people of the world.

At Midnight Mass the purple colours of Advent are replaced with white and gold. There are carols, music, flowers and candles as the Church family gathers to celebrate the birth of Jesus.

At home there are Christmas **cards, trees** and **presents**. They are signs of the good news of the coming of Jesus and of the love and care that we show to others because Jesus brings to us God's endless love and care.

Many cards are sold in aid of charities to help people in all kinds of need. The evergreen trees are a symbol of the everlasting life which is promised us with the coming of Jesus. The presents are signs of love and thoughtfulness for family and friends. In many churches children bring presents to the crib which are given to children in care or families in need.

A child has been born for us.
A son is given to us
and these are the
names he has been
given:
Strong friend,
Powerful God,
Ever-loving Father,
Bringer of peace.

Based on Isaiah 9:6-7
(See God's Story 3 p.59)

When the time was right,
God the Father sent Jesus into
the world.
Jesus had a mother just like
we do.
Jesus had to keep the rules
just like we do.
He came to let us know that we
are God's children too, in a
special way.
We are God's children, so we
can call God 'Abba', Father.

Based on Galatians 4:4-6
(See God's Story 2 p.88)

O little town of Bethlehem,
how still we see thee lie!
Above thy deep and dreamless sleep
the silent stars go by.
Yet, in thy dark streets shineth
the everlasting light;
the hopes and fears of all the
years
are met in thee tonight.

(Phillips Brooks 1835-93)

LENT

Lent is the Church's seasons for discerning and doing good.

In the Christian Year, Lent precedes and prepares for Easter. It is a penitential season and a time of spiritual growth. If people want to be followers of Jesus, they must be prepared to notice what others need and then see what they can do to help. During Lent this is traditionally put into practice through prayer, fasting and almsgiving. Christians make Lenten promises saying what they hope to do during Lent.

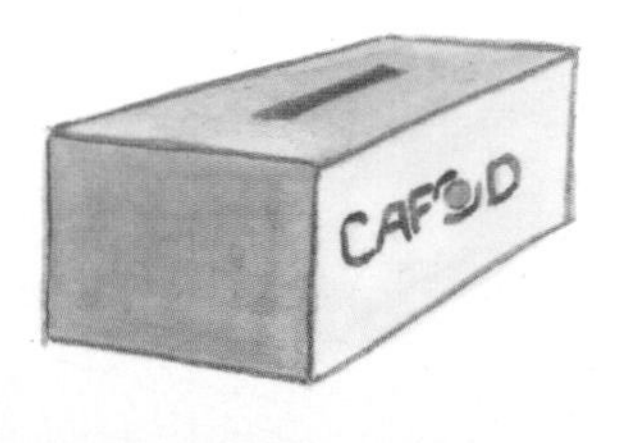

The Beatitudes – A New Way of Living
(based on Matthew 5: 1-17)

When he saw the crowds Jesus went up the mountain and sat down. His disciples gathered round him and this is what he taught them.

You will be blessed when you have an open and generous heart.
When you share what you have with other people
God will be very close to you.

You will be blessed when you reach out to those who grieve.
When you make friends with those who are sad and lonely,
God will be there to comfort you.

You will be blessed when you are gentle.
When you treat others with kindness and patience
God will give you all you need.

You will be blessed when you work for justice.
When you respect and stand up for the rights of others,
God will give you life to the full.

You will be blessed when you forgive others and don't hold grudges.
You will find God ready to forgive you.

You will be blessed when you desire what is good.
When you always search for what is good, you will find God in all around you.

You will be blessed when you are a peacemaker.
When you try not to let a quarrel even begin or are first to say sorry
you will be known as children of God.

You will be blessed when you are made fun of for doing what God wants.
When people laugh at you for living in God's way,
know that you are very close to God.
Remember what happened to so many of God's messengers.
Rejoice and be glad.

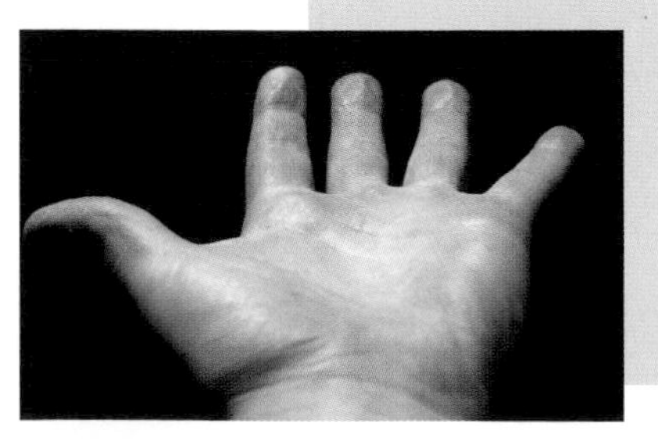

Taken from God's Story 3 p82

ASH WEDNESDAY

Ash Wednesday is the first day of Lent, the six weeks (forty days) set aside to prepare for Easter. During Lent, Christians try to make changes to their lives in order to become more like Jesus and live a new life of Easter joy. They search for ways in which they can live "good" lives and turn away from what is not "right". What people do during Lent helps them grow in holiness; growing in God's way.

Christians go to church on Ash Wednesday to receive ashes.

ASHES

The palms left over from last year's Palm/Passion Sunday are burned leaving the ashes. The priest blesses the ashes and prays: "*Lord God, bless all who ask for your forgiveness. Bless all those who receive these ashes. May they keep this Lenten season in preparation for the joy of Easter.*" The priest then makes a cross with the ashes on the forehead of everyone who comes in procession to the altar: he says, "*Turn away from sin and be faithful to the Gospel.*"

The Church family tries to do something extra during the 40 days of Lent:

Lent: a time for discernment

'To discern' means 'to gain insight'. During Lent Christians pray to gain understanding and strength in recognising 'good' and 'evil'. Like us Jesus was tempted, but he never chose to do what was bad. Because he was close to God his Father, he knew what the good response was. In the Gospel according to Luke, there is a story of a time when Jesus was tempted. You will find it in Luke 4:1-13 or in God's Story 3 p.94.

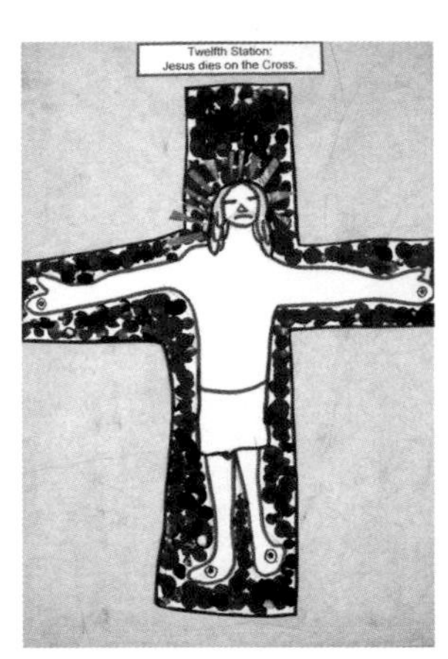

Pictures of the 2nd, 5th, 8th and 12th Stations of the Cross by St. Gregory's School, Northampton.

A prayer by Thomas a Kempis:

Grant me, O Lord,
to know what is worth knowing,
to love what is worth loving,
to praise what delights you most,
to value what is precious in your sight,
to hate what is offensive to you.
Do not let me judge by what I see,
nor pass sentence according to what I hear,
but to judge rightly between things that differ,
and above all to search out and do what pleases you,
through Jesus Christ our Lord.

(Good and Evil, Here I Am Years 4/5 and Years 5/6)

Lenten Devotions

A Way of the Cross: This is a special prayer for Christians, especially in Lent. It is also called Stations of the Cross. In church you will find 14 stations. Here is a shorter version you may like to use. Look up the references and name the events on the Way of the Cross.

1. John 19:16-17
2. Mark 15:21 3.
3. Luke 23:27-28
4. Luke 23:44-46
5. Luke 24:1-5;10-12.

(answers on p.126)

The Rosary

The five sorrowful mysteries of the Rosary help Christians to remember the sufferings of Jesus. These mysteries are: The Agony in the Garden; The Scourging at the Pillar; The Crowning with Thorns; The Carrying of the Cross; The Crucifixion and Death of Jesus. You may like to read the accounts of these events in the gospels or in God's Story 3 pp113-123.

(Growing, Here I Am Years 3/4 and 5/6)

HOLY WEEK

For the Church, the 'greatest week' is Holy Week during which the suffering, death and resurrection of Jesus is remembered in special celebrations. On Passion Sunday, which is sometimes called Palm Sunday, Christians go to church to celebrate Jesus' entrance into Jerusalem to face suffering and death.

Jesus was carried on a donkey into Jerusalem with the crowds of people waving their palm branches and shouting: "Hosanna! Praise God! Blessed is He who comes in the name of the Lord! Hosanna! Praise God!"

The people gather outside the church as the palms are blessed and distributed to everyone.
The story of Jesus' entry into Jerusalem is read from Scripture. Then the procession of people walks into the church, holding up palm crosses or green branches and singing hosannas.

The palms are twisted into the shape of a cross so that when they are taken home and displayed everyone will be reminded that the days of Holy Week lead up to the celebration of Good Friday when Jesus died on a cross.

Palm Sunday Around the World

clockwise from top: Jerusalem, Columbia, street procession in Ethiopia, children in El Salvador.

MAUNDY THURSDAY

Maundy Thursday is the Thursday of Holy Week, the final week of Lent. During this Holy Week Jesus' complete self-giving is remembered by Christians in the liturgies of the Easter Triduum - (Holy Thursday, Good Friday and Holy Saturday). Throughout Holy Week/Lent the church statues and crucifixes are covered in purple cloths. There are no flowers and the Alleluia is not sung. These symbols remind the Church family of the 'dying' in order to celebrate the 'new life' of Easter.

MASS OF THE LORD'S SUPPER

On Maundy Thursday evening the Church family remembers Jesus giving himself to his friends at the Last Supper and the giving of himself to his enemies in Gethsemane to be crucified.

During the Mass of the Lord's Supper the Church family remembers how Jesus washed his friends' feet as they prepared to celebrate together. Peter was unhappy at first but Jesus ordered the apostles to follow his example. This is why the parish priest follows Jesus' example and washes the feet of twelve parishioners. The Pope traditionally washes the feet of twelve people in Rome. This symbolises the self-giving Jesus asks of those who follow him.

Christian leaders follow the example of Jesus and reenact the washing of the feet.
Centre: Pope Benedict XVI in St Peter's, Rome
Left: The Anglican Archbishop of Canterbury

The Mass on this evening calls to mind the first time Jesus gave himself to his friends in a very special way. This is known as the institution of the Eucharist. The night before he died Jesus shared a "Last Supper" with his friends. He took the bread, blessed it and broke it and said "*Take this and eat it, this is my body*". Then he took the wine, blessed it and said "*Take this and drink it, this is my blood*". Then he asked the apostles to do the same thing in memory of him.

Because this Maundy Thursday Mass is a special celebration the priest wears white vestments. The Gloria is sung and bells are rung.

The priest takes the Blessed Sacrament to a special place where people keep watch. This reminds them of Jesus praying in the garden of Gethsemane and asking his friends to 'keep watch with me'. When Mass is over, the altar is stripped bare and the tabernacle is left empty.

Jesus the giver

Jesus was always giving of himself. Whenever people needed him, he was there with all the time in the world to give to them. He gave them the best example by the way he lived his life.

On Maundy Thursday Christians listen to the story of the last supper Jesus shared with his friends. He taught them by his actions and his words how they were to be givers like him.

Words of the Eucharist

This is my body which will be given for you. This is my blood which will be poured out for you.

Prayers during the washing of feet

If I, your Lord and Teacher,
have washed your feet, then surely
you must wash one another's feet.
If there is this love among you,
all will know that you are my
disciples.
I give you a new commandment:
Love one another as I have
loved you.

GOOD FRIDAY

Good Friday is the second day of the Easter Triduum. This is a solemn day when the people gather together in Church to remember the suffering and death of Jesus. He was taken to a place called Golgotha in Jerusalem and crucified. According to tradition Jesus died at 3 o'clock in the afternoon so this is when the Church invites everyone to take part in the reading of the "*Passion of Jesus*" from the Gospel of John.

Many prayers are also said for the needs of the church and the whole world because Jesus died for everyone.

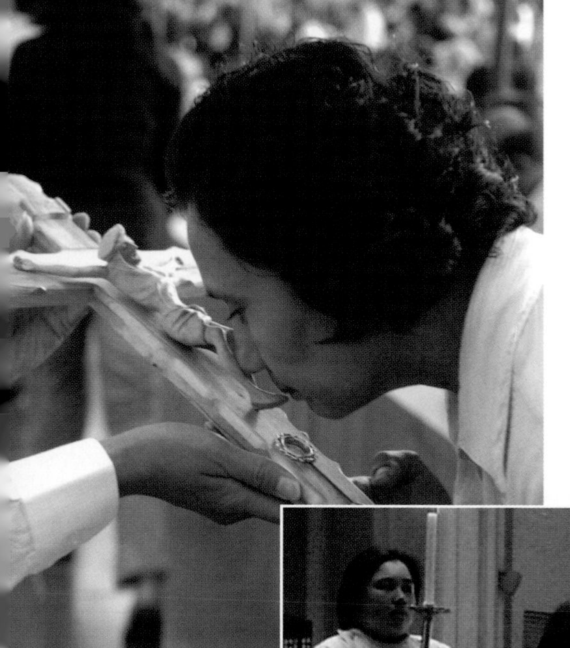

The priest removes a purple cloth from the wooden crucifix, holds it up and prays:

This is the wood of the cross on which hung the Saviour of the world.

Then people are invited to come up in procession to touch or kiss the cross while a penitential psalm is sung.

Everyone joins in the Lord's Prayer and then receives Holy Communion. There is a silence at the end of the liturgy as people leave the church, stripped bare of all decoration.

Stations of the Cross
Above: on the Via Dolorosa in Jerusalem
Below: in Times Square, New York

On Good Friday
The reading of the passion of Jesus according to John is an important part of the Good Friday Liturgy. These are some of the people who have a place in the events. You may want to find out more about them.

Simon Peter
John tells us about what Simon Peter did in the garden when Jesus was arrested and what happened later at the high priest's house. How do you think this helped Peter to become a better disciple?

Pontius Pilate
The Roman governor was puzzled by Jesus and wanted to set him free. Why do you think he did not free Jesus?

The Women
John names three women who stood near the cross of Jesus. Who are they?

The Disciple
One disciple who was there with the women is named. Who is he? What did Jesus ask him to do?

Joseph of Arimathaea and Nicodemus

Both were disciples in secret, but when Jesus died they showed their love and respect. How did they do this?

Good Friday processions around the world

Below: 1. Jerusalem, 2. El Salvador, 3. Pope John Paul II leads a Good Friday service in the Colosseum in Rome, 4. France, 5. Costa Rica Opposite page: Good Friday in Guatemala.

Above: carrying a procession float through the streets Colourful 'carpets' are laid in the streets. On the left made of sawdust and below of flowers.

THE EASTER VIGIL

Easter begins on Holy Saturday night when there is a special vigil. 'To keep vigil' is 'to keep watch' during the night. The Church had accompanied Jesus through his suffering and death and now waits to share and celebrate his new life. Inside and outside the church all is darkness. Christians everywhere are waiting for the moment when they pass from darkness to light, from the discipline of Lent to the joy of Easter. The actions, prayers and symbols used during this vigil tell the Easter story.

New Fire

Everyone gathers outside the church. The priest blesses the new fire. It is a symbol of Jesus who passes from death to life.

The Easter Candle

Next the priest blesses the Easter candle and lights it from the new fire. The candle is a special Easter symbol, a sign of Jesus, the light of the world and the new life which he shares. The church too is being renewed. He prays: "*May the light of Christ, rising in glory, dispel the darkness of our hearts and minds.*"

The deacon or priest leads the people into the darkness of the church. He stops three times to sing: 'Christ our Light' and everyone responds 'Thanks be to God'.

Then the light from the Easter candle is spread all through the church and everyone holds a lighted candle. This symbolises the Good News of Jesus' resurrection which is to be shared by everyone present and by the whole world.

The deacon or priest sings a special Easter song of praise to proclaim the good news 'Jesus Christ, our King, is risen!' This is called the Exsultet.

Pilgrims in Jerusalem, sharing the Light of Christ.

THE LITURGY OF THE WORD

Everyone sits down to listen to the story of God's love that began with the creation of the world and is shown most clearly in the life, death and resurrection of Jesus.

The readings from the Old Testament all emphasise the unfailing and steadfast love of God. The number of readings may be changed, but the reading from the book of Exodus about the passover of the Israelites from slavery to freedom is always included. Another favourite reading is from the prophet Ezekiel who encourages God's people with this promise. God says:

"I am going to gather you together and
bring you home.
I will pour clean water over you and you will be
clean again.
I will make you new again and you will be
full of love.
I will put my Spirit in you and you will do
what is right.
You will be my people and I will be your God."

Based on Ezekiel 36:24-28 (See God's Story 3 p.66)

Blessing the Easter Candle

As the priest blesses the candle he draws the sign of the cross and near this the figures for the year. For example, 2005. As he does this he says:

Christ yesterday and today
the beginning and the end,
Alpha and Omega
all time belongs to him
and all the ages;
to him be glory and power
through every age and for ever.
Amen.

He also puts five grains of incense in the form of a cross and says:
By his holy
and glorious wounds
may Christ our Lord
guard us
and keep us.
Amen
(Death/New Life, Here I Am Years 5/6)

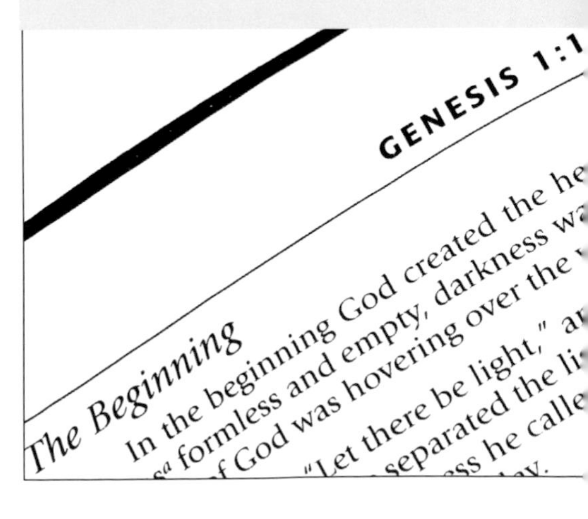

THE MASS OF EASTER NIGHT

After the last reading from the Old Testament the candles are lit on the altar. The singing of the 'Glory to God' tonight is accompanied with the ringing of bells and playing of music because this is the first time the Gloria has been sung during mass, since the beginning of Lent, with the exception of Holy Thursday. Everyone praises, blesses and thanks God for the risen Christ.

After the first reading from the New Testament the priest or deacon sings 'Alleluia' for the first time since the beginning of Lent to prepare for the proclamation of the Gospel.

Baptism Liturgy
This Easter Mass is the time when adults or older children are baptised and confirmed and received into the Church.

The priest blesses water using a long and beautiful blessing which traces the powerful symbol of water from the '*dawn of creation' to* the baptism of Jesus Christ and all his followers. When the water is blessed the priest lowers the Easter candle into the water of the baptismal font and lifts it out again. The action symbolises the death, burial and resurrection of Jesus. He calls on the Holy Spirit to fill the water with God's power and love. He prays: "*May all who are buried with Christ in the death of baptism rise also with him to newness of life.*"

If there are no baptisms the water is still blessed and the people's candles are relit. Holding their lighted candles the people renew their baptismal promises and profess their faith in God the Father, the Son and the Holy Spirit. The priest sprinkles everyone with the holy water.

The Mass continues and the newly baptised are usually the first to receive Holy Communion.

Alleluia, alleluia
At the end of Mass the deacon or priest sings:
The Mass is ended, go in peace, alleluia, alleluia.
Everyone responds:
Thanks be to God, alleluia, alleluia.

EASTER SUNDAY

Easter Sunday is the beginning of the Easter Season which lasts for 50 days. All through Easter week the double 'Alleluia' at the end of Mass is a symbol of Easter joy. Jesus is risen and shares his new life. The priest wears white vestments and spring flowers in church are another sign of new life.

Prayer after Communion for Ascension day

Father,
in this Eucharist
we touch the divine life
you give to the world.
Help us to follow Christ
with love
to eternal life where he is Lord
for ever and ever.
Amen.

ASCENSION

Forty days after Easter the Church celebrates the feast of the Ascension of the Lord. In the Acts of the Apostles Luke tells how Jesus appeared to his disciples teaching them about the kingdom of God. The four gospels tell of different events, but they agree that the apostles did not recognise Jesus straightaway and found it hard to believe he was truly alive.

The New Testament says that Jesus went back to God his Father. At that time people thought that God's home in heaven was 'up above'. Jesus said he was going back to his Father. He promised his friends that he himself, the Father and the Spirit would always be present among those who believed in him. He said, "We will make our home in you."

The feast of the Ascension is celebrated in the Easter season when the Church is thinking about the joy of the new life Jesus shares with the world. The prayers of the feast remind us that, through Baptism and the Eucharist, Jesus shares his life with us now.

In the Acts of the Apostles, Luke tells how Jesus, before he returned to his Father, said to his friends, "Go out to the whole world and proclaim the Good News to everyone." (Mark 16:15,16)

Jesus promised to send the Holy Spirit to help them to do this. They were to wait in Jerusalem for his promise to be fulfilled.

PENTECOST

At Mass today the priest wears red vestments. Many churches put up special banners and symbols of the Holy Spirit to remind everyone of the gifts of the Spirit. The Church celebrates the fulfilment of Jesus' promise that the Holy Spirit would guide and help his disciples to understand all that he had taught them.

Pentecost is sometimes called the 'birthday' of the Church. In the Acts of the Apostles Luke recounts how the apostles all gathered together with Mary, the mother of Jesus. They felt dejected. Jesus had promised never to leave them and yet he was gone from them. He had said he would send them another friend to help them, but they didn't know quite what he meant. On the day of Pentecost, the feast of the first fruits, they knew Jesus had kept his promise.

They described the coming of the Spirit as being like a mighty wind and tongues of fire. They were filled with the Spirit of Jesus, a spirit of joy, love, happiness and peace. They wanted to share their happiness with everyone. They stopped being afraid and went out into the streets to begin to tell everyone about Jesus and the good news of his life and death and new risen life. They found that they could communicate with people from many different parts of the world who had come to Jerusalem for the feast. That is how the Church began. So Pentecost is the beginning, the birthday of the Church.

Some parishes make this a day to celebrate the richness and diversity of the parish family. Just as the disciples found joy in the gift of different tongues, so today is a good time to remember the different languages people in the parish and neighbourhood speak. It is a time to celebrate the richness of the different cultures of the worldwide Catholic family.

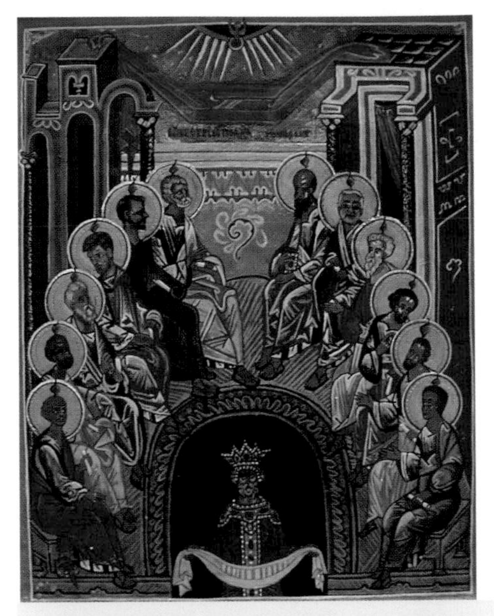

The Gifts of the Spirit
Wisdom
Understanding
Right Judgement
Courage
Knowledge
Reverence
Wonder and Awe in God's Presence
(Initiation, Here I Am Years 5/6)

The fruit of these gifts is seen in communities where there is love, joy, peace, patience, kindness, goodness, faithfulness, gentleness and self-control.

Peace Everywhere
Peace
Pax
Shalom
Paix
Pace
How many languages do you think people speak in your parish?

FEASTS TO CELEBRATE

The Church's year is a journey with Jesus through the events of his life, death and resurrection. As well as the seasons of Advent, Lent and Easter there are special feast days throughout the year. These remind Christians of the many different ways in which Jesus makes the whole of life holy for those who believe in him.

Trinity Sunday

On the Sunday after the feast of Pentecost, the Church celebrates what Jesus revealed to the world about God, Father, Son and Holy Spirit, the Holy Trinity. This is one of the 'mysteries' of faith which can only be understood with God's help and the gift of faith. The sign of the cross is a profession of faith in the Holy Trinity which Christians use every day. It is a reminder that always and everywhere God is with us.

The Body and Blood of Christ

This feast is celebrated on the Thursday after Trinity Sunday. It's Latin name is 'Corpus Christi'. It is a celebration of Jesus' gift of himself in the Eucharist and in Holy Communion. In some countries there are processions and the Blessed Sacrament is carried through the streets. It is a traditional time for children to make their first Holy Communion.

The Sacred Heart of Jesus

In many cultures the heart is a symbol of love. This feast is celebrated on the Friday after the Second Sunday of Pentecost. The feast celebrates the faithful and everlasting love of Jesus for every person. The Church remembers Jesus' words to his disciples, " A new commandment I give you, that you love one another as I have loved you." (John 13:34)

Names

A number of churches and schools in England and Wales take their name from these feasts. Jesus is their example. Many churches and schools are named after a saint.

When does your church or school celebrate its special feast day?

(For the Church's Year see Journeys, Here I Am Years 3/4 and 5/6)

Christ the King

This feast is celebrated on the last Sunday of Ordinary Time, the Sunday before the first Sunday of Advent. It is a celebration of the power of Jesus to set all people free from sin and death, free to live for ever. He did this by his life, his death on the cross and his resurrection. This reminds Christians that Jesus said his kingship was about service. At the last supper he washed the feet of his disciples and said, "If I, your Lord and Teacher, have washed your feet, you also ought to wash one another's feet. For I have set you an example, that you also should do as I have done to you." (John 13:14-15)

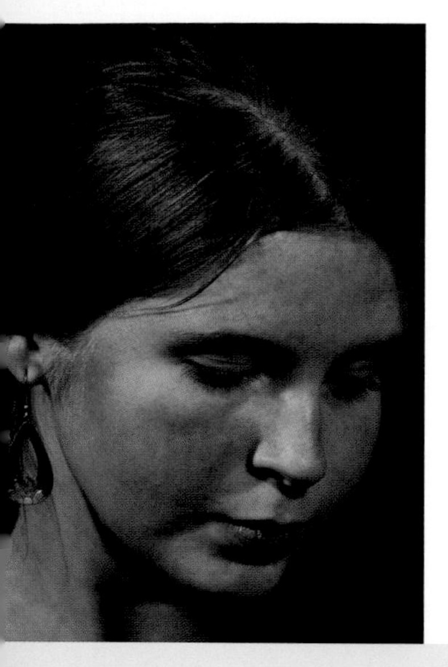

MARY

Mary the Mother of Jesus has a special place in the Church's seasons and feasts. In Advent the Church celebrates her 'Yes' to God and her example of preparing for the coming of Jesus. On Good Friday the Church celebrates her love and faithfulness as she stood at the foot of the cross. For the Church, May is Mary's month and in October Catholics are encouraged to pray the Rosary. There are also special feasts through the year and many local traditions and celebrations throughout the world.

The Rosary

The Rosary is a special prayer used by Christians. It used to be called Our Lady's Psalter because it is really a journey with Mary through the life of Jesus. It has twenty steps or decades. To pray a decade you say one 'Our Father', ten 'Hail Marys' and one 'Glory Be'.

Mary
Mary was with Jesus from the beginning to the end of his life journey. Christians pray that she will share their life journey with the same motherly love.

(Journeys, Here I Am Years 3/4 and 5/6)

The repetition of the prayers is a way of freeing yourself from busy thoughts and fixing your attention on Jesus just as Mary, his mother, often would have done. The twenty steps are made up of five joyful, five sorrowful and five glorious times in the lives of Jesus and Mary. In 2003 Pope John Paul II invited the Church to pray five Mysteries of Light:. These are events in the life of Jesus when his disciples began to understand who he was.

The Baptism of Jesus: "You are my beloved Son in whom I am well pleased."
The Wedding-feast at Cana: "Do whatever he tells you."
The proclamation of the kingdom in the sermon on the mount: "Blessed are ..."
The Transfiguration: "This is my Son, the Beloved, listen to him."
The gift of the Eucharist at the last supper: "This is my Body. This is my Blood."

The Mysteries of the Rosary
'Mysteries' are events in the life of Jesus which we need God's help to understand.

Joyful
Annunciation
Visitation
Nativity
Presentation in the Temple
Finding in the Temple

Mysteries of Light
Baptism of Jesus
Marriage Feast of Cana
Proclamation of the Kingdom
The Transfiguration
The Gift of the Eucharist

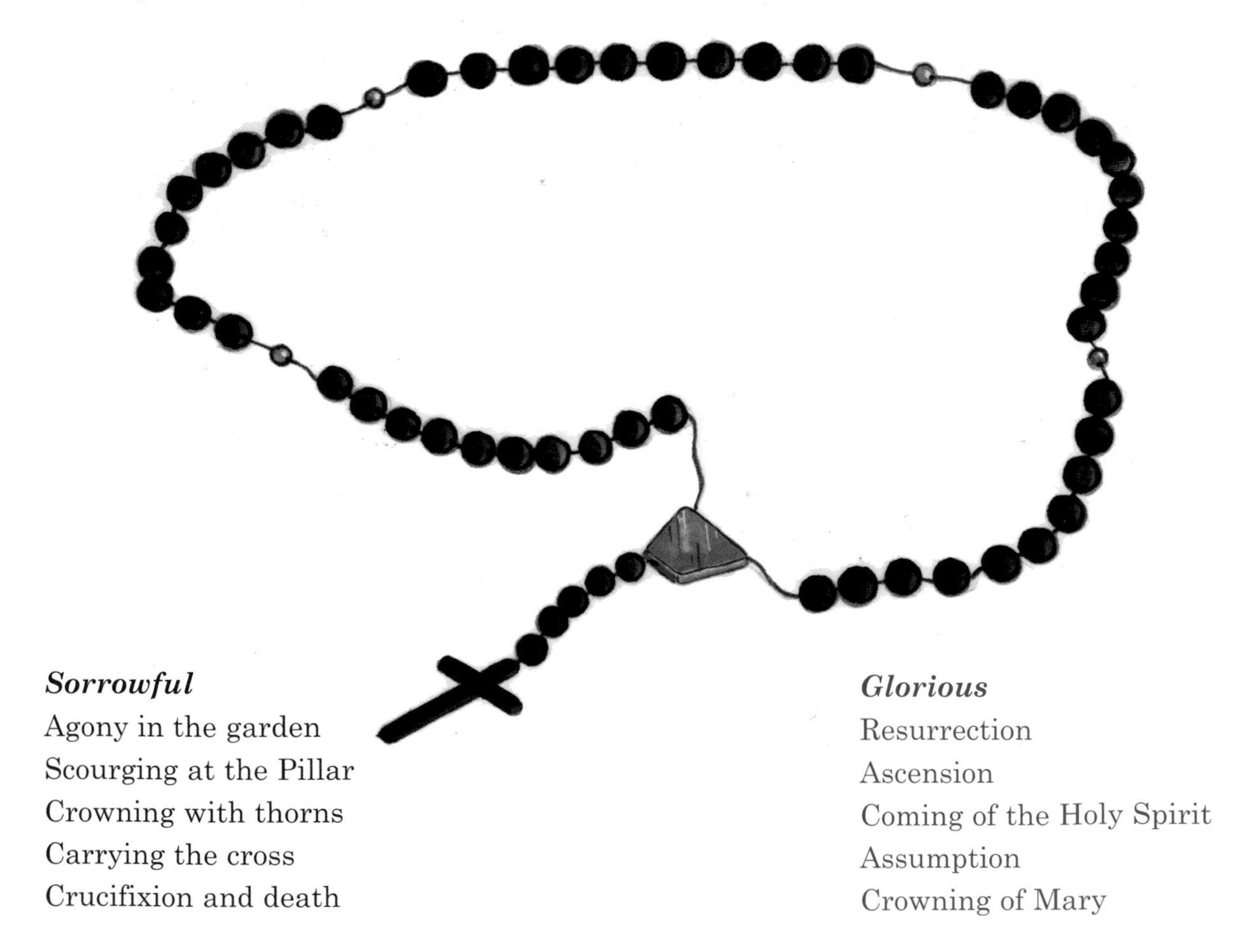

Sorrowful
Agony in the garden
Scourging at the Pillar
Crowning with thorns
Carrying the cross
Crucifixion and death

Glorious
Resurrection
Ascension
Coming of the Holy Spirit
Assumption
Crowning of Mary

God's Work of Art

In a very special way Mary is God's work of art. Alone of creation she lived the good life, as from the beginning she was called by God to live it. Like all works of art she was irreplaceable... full of grace.

(Praying the Rosary, David Konstant, Collins 1981)

These are six of the many feasts the Church celebrates in honour of Mary

Mary the Mother of God
This feast is celebrated on New Year's Day, 1st January. The Church honours Mary as Mother of Jesus and Mother of God.

The Annunciation
This feast on the 25th March honours Mary's love and faithfulness, when she said 'Yes' to becoming the mother of Jesus. From the gospel of St Luke come the words of God's messenger, Gabriel, "Hail, full of grace, the Lord is with you." These have become part of the Church's prayer the Hail Mary

The Visitation
The feast on the 31st May celebrates Mary's visit to her cousin Elizabeth. It is Elizabeth's words from the gospel of Luke that have become the second part of of the Hail Mary: "Blessed are you among women and blessed is the fruit of your womb."

The Assumption
This feast celebrates that when Mary died she went straight to Heaven, her body as well as her spirit. The feast is celebrated on the 15th August.

Mary's birthday
No one knows when Mary was born but the Church celebrates her birthday on the 8th September. This is one of only three birthdays that the Church celebrates. The others are the birth of Jesus and the birth of John the Baptist, Elizabeth's son and Jesus' cousin. For all other saints the Church celebrates the day of their death as their birthday into eternal life.

The Immaculate Conception
On the 8th December the Church celebrates this feast of God's special gift by which Mary was full of grace from the very beginning of her life.

ALL SAINTS

All through the year the Church celebrates men, women and children who have loved and served God by holy lives. The Church canonises them which means they are called saints and the Church believes that they are with God and know God's love fully and perfectly. On page 33 of this book you read about the 'Communion of Saints', the collective name given to all members of the Church community whether living or dead. Not all of them are canonised saints, many are Christians whose love and goodness were known only to their families and friends and to God.

The Church celebrates 'All the Saints' on 1st November. It is a day to remember all the love and kindness of the saints we have known and loved.

ALL THE FAITHFUL DEPARTED

The next day, 2nd November, the Church celebrates the feast of All the Faithful Departed. We believe that everyone who dies goes to God, but we don't know exactly what this means. St Paul says after we die we will see God as God truly is and that God is light. Christians believe that God is eternal, that means not measured by time as we are, so when we pray for those who die we pray that they may share God's eternal life and light. It is a day to pray for all who have died, not just people we know, and especially those who may have no one to pray for them.

Prayer for those who have died

Eternal rest grant to them O Lord and let perpetual light shine upon them

Welcome

Dear Friends,

Within these pages is a Story which continues. It is a story in which we all have a part to play. It is the *Church's Story* and it helps us to recognise the ways in which it is lived and told, from generation to generation, week after week, year after year.

It helps us to recognise ourselves as the People of God celebrating significant moments in the Church's history and our own. Within the three sections of this book we find the community of the Church as it gathers, the Sacraments which give their gathering meaning and the celebrations of Christian Life which form the pattern of the Church's year. The first section sees the community gathered in home, school and parish. The second section unfolds these gatherings to present the sacraments that draw the community together. And the third section includes the celebrations of the particular events in the life of Jesus and the life of the Early Church.

Church's Story is a companion volume to *God's Story*, a scriptural resource for Foundation and Key stages 1&2, and complements the Religious Education resource *Here I Am*.

In homes, schools and parishes I am sure this portrayal of the Church's Tradition will be an invaluable resource for teachers, catechists, ministers of the Word for children and parents. The Church's Story lives on in you and in the children in your care.
May you be enriched by its living and sharing.

† Edwin Regan
Bishop of Wrexham
Chairman of the National Project

Introduction

The Church teaches that Catholic life and teaching is formed, nourished and deepened by Scripture and Tradition.

In the Scriptures God speaks. The Church teaches that in the word of God the good news of the love of the Father revealed in the Son by the power of the Holy Spirit is proclaimed for all the peoples of the world. Tradition is the living transmission of this good news by the apostles who were formed and taught by Jesus Christ and their successors. This 'handing-on' has continued from generation to generation by the whole Church, the body of Christ. The Holy Spirit "through whom the living voice of the Gospel rings out in the Church – and through her in the world – leads believers to the full truth, and makes the Word of Christ dwell in them in all its richness." (CCC 79)

The Church's Story – lived by the People of God introduces children to this lived Tradition. It complements *God's Story,* the Scripture resource first published in 2002.

The Church's Story 1 is for the very youngest children.

The Church's Story 2 is for ages 5-7.

The Church's Story 3 is for ages 8-11 and beyond.

The three books offer progression in language, style of presentation and extent of text.

Where and how children learn

In their communities of home, school and parish, children have opportunities to experience the community life, sacramental celebrations and the seasons and feasts of the Church's year. Through these experiences, their knowledge and understanding are deepened.

What children learn in these books

Children will learn about:

- the Church – the community of believers living and sharing Christian faith at home, in the parish community and in the world-wide family of the Church;
- the Sacraments – how God's love and presence are revealed and celebrated in the Church's sacraments;
- the Christian life of love, self-giving and service which is celebrated, experienced, reflected upon and expressed year by year in the liturgical cycle of seasons and feasts.

Teachers and catechists will recognise in this structure the three kinds of Themes of *Here I Am* and *Walk with Me.*

These Notes for Adults offer background information and practical suggestions to help all those who share these books with younger children to encourage their understanding and learning.

Notes for Adults

The Church:
The People of God (pp.8-35)

This section supports teaching and learning as children develop knowledge and understanding about Church as the Family (the Domestic Church), the Community (Local Church of diocese and parish) and World Family (Universal Church).

The focus is shaped by Christian faith that God the Creator calls each person to life; that Jesus, the Son of God made man, reveals God, his Father, and how people are to live as children of God; and that by the power of the Holy Spirit, Christians through space and time become one family – one in the love of Father, Son and Holy Spirit and one in loving, self-giving and service of one another and of the world and its peoples.

Among the key skills to be developed and fostered in this area of learning are:

- ability to name and celebrate good in self and others;
- ability to identify and describe the practice and faith of a community;
- ability to discern and raise questions about living in the human community.

Among the key attitudes to be fostered in this area of learning are:

- respect for self, others and God the Creator;
- respect and reverence for faith and tradition;
- willingness to value diversity and the gifts of the Spirit.

Talk and Think

Some questions to explore with children:

Looking at creation (pp.8-11 and 16-19)

Which of the photos of animals did you like best? Why?

Where have you seen the variety and beauty of the world?

How do you feel about being unique?

What made you glad about the uniqueness of another person?

How does every person being unique challenge us?

What are some of the ways in which the people in other parts of the world contribute to the way you live?

What are some of the ways in which you and your family contribute to the way of life people in other parts of the world?

What are some of the benefits of being 'One World'?

What are some of the challenges to being 'One World'?

Looking at family life (pp. 12-15)

Look at the pictures of families around the world and think about your family life. What is the same? What is different?

What are some of the best things about family life?

What are some of the challenges?

Looking at the Church and its mission (pp.20-35)

Questions for this section will be found with the pictures. Some further areas to explore:

When have you enjoyed being part of a community?

When have you enjoyed being part of the Church family?

Why might someone decide to go on pilgrimage?

What joys and challenges would they face?

The Church's Sacraments (pp.36-79)

This section supports teaching and learning as children develop knowledge and understanding about the seven sacraments of the Catholic Church. The focus is shaped by Catholic faith that in the sacraments Christ is present and by the power of the Holy Spirit graces us to live the love of the Father that was revealed and communicated in the Paschal mystery – his life, death and resurrection.

"The challenge of Christian discipleship is to take the Incarnation seriously; to believe that following Jesus who is 'the way, the truth and the life' affects every aspect of our daily lives; and to believe that in our ordinary loving relationships we are sharing in the very life of God, the Father, Son and Holy Spirit." (Here I Am, Teacher's Information p.14)

Children learn about the signs and symbols of the sacramental liturgies which embody Catholic teaching that "The liturgy of the Church presupposes, integrates and sanctifies elements from creation and human culture, conferring on them the dignity of signs of grace, of the new creation in Jesus Christ." (CCC,1149).

For each sacrament a double page spread acts as a summary by asking: What will you see? What will you hear? Who will be there? What will be happening? Teachers may find this useful for diagnostic, formative and summative assessment.

Among the key skills to be developed and fostered in this area of learning are:

- ability to listen and to make a response;
- ability to relate in friendship and love;
- ability to examine and identify issues of right and wrong.

Among the key attitudes to be fostered in this area of learning are:

- openness to being involved;
- willingness to search for meaning beyond the immediate and material.
- respect for truth and confidence to live the truth.

Talk and Think

Questions to explore with children should be shaped by the general approach: the action of God, the links to the life, death and resurrection of Jesus and the signs and symbols.

'God says 'Here I Am. I am with you and I love you' as proposed on p.37.

For example: How might [new parents, a new Christian, someone who is sick, someone who has got into trouble, a person getting married, a new priest] feel at this time? Why might they be glad to know God is present to love and guide them?

The significance of the signs and symbols of each sacrament within human culture

For example: What are some other ways/times when people use [water, oil, greetings, promises, meals]? Why is it important to express [thanks, love, forgiveness]?

Links to Jesus and the gospels

It might be useful to refer to God's Story, the complementary resource for Church's Story and read the appropriate section. For example, the baptism of Jesus, the Last Supper, Jesus' promise to be with his friends always.

Christian Living:
The Church's Year (pp.80-119)

This section supports teaching and learning as children develop knowledge and understanding about the liturgical year and its cycle of seasons and feasts: Advent and Christmas, Lent and Easter, Pentecost – the gift of the Holy Spirit for the mission of the Church.

The focus is shaped by Catholic faith that 'in the liturgical year the various aspects of the one Paschal mystery unfold' (CCC,1171). The signs and symbols of the seasons and feast are emphasised, as are the fruits of the Holy Spirit which the celebration of the various seasons develop – love and joy in loving, self-control and self-giving, generosity and compassion in serving others and commitment to living the good news.

Among the key skills to be developed and fostered in this area of learning are:

- ability to make connections between celebrations and the Church season and feast;
- ability to describe the symbols and spirit of the Church season and feast;
- use empathy to describe belief and a faith response.

Among the key attitudes to be fostered in this area of learning are:

- a sense of wonder and joy;
- openness to the challenge of the sacrifice of Jesus;
- openness to the gift of freedom and the Holy Spirit.

Talk and Think

The questions explored should seek to deepen children's understanding of the life of Jesus, the significance of the signs and symbols the Church uses and the role of the season/feast in Christian living.

Links to the life of Christ

For example: What event in the life of Jesus is being celebrated? Why is it important to remember this?

The significance of signs and symbols of the season/feast and their relation to human culture

For example: What changes in your life/ your family life mark the seasons of the year [spring, summer, winter]? What are some of the symbols which signify a birthday celebration? Why is the Easter candle important?

The significance of the season/feast for Christian life and human development

For example: Explore 'waiting' in Advent - Do you find it hard to wait? When is waiting good? Explore self-control in Lent – How can exercise help people? Why do some people find it hard to exercise even when they know it's good to do?

Way of the Cross p99

Answers: 1 Jesus receives his cross; 2 Simon helps Jesus; 3 Jesus meets the women; 4 Jesus dies on the cross; 5 Jesus is risen

Picture credits

1	Empics
p.6	istockphoto International
p.8	Dreamstime Picture Source
p.9	Dreamstime Picture Source
p.10	istockphoto International
p.11	istockphoto International
p.12	istockphoto International
p.13	Empics
p.13	istockphoto International
p.14	istockphoto International
p.15	istockphoto International
p.16	Dreamstime Picture Source
p.17	Corbis Picture Library, London
p.18	Painent Picture Library
p.19	Painent Picture Library
p.20	Illustration: Kati Teague
p.21	Corbis Picture Library, London
p.21	Painent Picture Library
p.22	Corbis Picture Library, London
p.22	istockphoto International
p.22	Painent Picture Library
p.23	Corbis Picture Library, London
p.23	istockphoto International
p.23	Painent Picture Library
p.24	St George's Parish, Warminster, photo Olivia Antolik
p.25	St George's Parish, Warminster, photo Olivia Antolik
p.25	St Nicholas of Tolentino Parish, Bristol, photo Olivia Antolik
p.28	Empics
p.29	Corbis Picture Library, London
p.29	istockphoto International
p.30	© Bibleplaces.com
p.31	© Bibleplaces.com
p.31	Lumière du monde, France
p.34	The Forty Martyr-Saints of England and Wales, Society of Jesus
p.36	St Nicholas of Tolentino Parish, Bristol, photo Olivia Antolik
p.36	Photo by Randy Redford © St. James Cathedral, Seattle
p.36	Photo by Randy Redford © St. James Cathedral, Seattle
p.37	Catholic News Service
p.37	Dreamstime Picture Source
p.37	St Nicholas of Tolentino Parish, Bristol, photo Olivia Antolik
p.37	© St James Cathedral, Seattle
p.40	photo Olivia Antolik
pp.46-49	photos © St. Anne's, Union City, California
pp.52-63	St Nicholas of Tolentino Parish, Bristol & St George's Parish, Warminster, photos Olivia Antolik
p.66	istockphoto International
p.66	St George's Parish, Warminster, photo Olivia Antolik
p.67	St George's Parish, Warminster, photo Olivia Antolik
p.70	Catholic News Service
p.70	Lumière du monde, France

p.70 St George's Parish, Warminster, photo Olivia Antolik
p.71 Catholic News Service
p.71 Corbis Picture Library, London
p.75 Dreamstime Picture Source
p.76 Dreamstime Picture Source
p.77 istockphoto International
p.80 Ordination of Philip Beisly Tom Smith Mark Moran, Clifton Cathedral. photo Oliver Reutter
p.81 Ordination of Christopher Warren and Mark Millward, photo Diocese of Hexham & Newcastle
p.82 Ordination of Christopher Warren and Mark Millward, photo Diocese of Hexham & Newcastle
p.82 Ordination of Philip Beisly Tom Smith Mark Moran, Clifton Cathedral. photo Oliver Reutter
p.83 Ordination of Philip Beisly Tom Smith Mark Moran, Clifton Cathedral. photo Oliver Reutter
p.85 Illustration Kati Teague
p.86 Illustration Kati Teague
p.87 Illustration Kati Teague
p.88 istockphoto International
p.89 istockphoto International
p.90 istockphoto International
p.90 Illustration Kati Teague
p.91 Illustration Kati Teague
p.92 photo © St James Cathedral, Seattle
p.93 Illustration Kati Teague
p.93 photo © St James Cathedral, Seattle
p.94 Illustration Kati Teague
p.94 photo © St James Cathedral, Seattle
p.95 Dreamstime Picture Source
p.95 istockphoto International
p.96 istockphoto International
p.97 Artist: Ulrich Henn. Photo © St. James Cathedral, Seattle
p.98 istockphoto International
p.99 St Gregory's Catholic Primary School, Northampton
p.100 istockphoto International
p.100 photo © St James Cathedral, Seattle
p.101 Corbis Picture Library, London
p.102 Empics
p.102 Lumière du monde, France
p.103 Artist: Ulrich Henn, 2003. Photo © St. James Cathedral, Seattle
p.104 photo © St James Cathedral, Seattle
p.105 Corbis Picture Library, London
p.108 Dreamstime Picture Source
p.108 Empics
p.109 Corbis Picture Library, London
p.110 Photo by Randy Redford © St. James Cathedral, Seattle
p.111 Dreamstime Picture Source
p.111 istockphoto International
p.112 Artist: Hans Gottfried von Stockhausen, photo © St James Cathedral, Seattle
p.113 Artist: Joan Brand-Landkamer, photo © St James Cathedral, Seattle
p.114 istockphoto International
p.114 photo © St James Cathedral, Seattle
p.115 Dreamstime Picture Source
p.116 Dreamstime Picture Source
p.117 Illustration Kati Teague
p.118 istockphoto International